Better Homes and Gardens®

STRETCHING
LIVING SPACE

BETTER HOMES AND GARDENS® BOOKS

Editor: Gerald M. Knox
Art Director: Ernest Shelton
Managing Editor: David A. Kirchner

Associate Art Director (Managing): Randall Yontz
Associate Art Directors (Creative): Linda Ford, Neoma Alt West
Copy and Production Editors: Nancy Nowiszewski,
Lamont Olson, Mary Helen Schiltz, David A. Walsh
Assistant Art Directors: Harijs Priekulis, Tom Wegner
Graphic Designers: Mike Burns, Alisann Dixon, Mike Eagleton,
Lynda Haupert, Deb Miner, Lyne Neymeyer, Trish Church-
Podlasek, Stan Sams, D. Greg Thompson, Darla Whipple,
Paul Zimmerman

Editor in Chief: Neil Kuehnl
Group Editorial Services Director: Duane L. Gregg

General Manager: Fred Stines
Director of Publishing: Robert B. Nelson
Director of Retail Marketing: Jamie Martin
Director of Direct Marketing: Arthur Heydendael

All About Your House: Stretching Living Space

Project Editor: James A. Hufnagel
Associate Project Editor: Walter D. Brownfield
Assistant Editor: Leonore A. Levy
Copy and Production Editor: David A. Walsh
Building and Remodeling Editor: Joan McCloskey
Furnishings and Design Editor: Shirley Van Zante
Garden and Outdoor Living Editor: Beverly Garrett
Money Management and Features Editor: Margaret Daly

Art Director: Linda Ford
Graphic Designer: Mike Eagleton

Contributors: David Ashe, Carolyn Bishop, James Downing,
Paul Krantz, Jean LemMon, William L. Nolan, Jerry Reedy,
Marcia Spires

Special thanks to William N. Hopkins, Bill Hopkins, Babs Klein,
and Don Wipperman for their valuable contributions to this book.

STRETCHING
LIVING
SPACE

INTRODUCTION

Space—few homes ever seem to have quite enough of it. And though most of us know we can put the rooms in our houses to better use, often it's difficult to figure out just how. Maybe you simply need the *illusion* of more space that deft decorating can create. Or should you try to fit more function into existing rooms? Reshuffle partitions? Finish off basement, attic, or garage space? Bump out with a greenhouse, bay, or porch enclosure?

Stretching Living Space systematically examines all the ways—short of a major addition—your house can live bigger. It begins with a room-by-room analysis of your family's space needs; presents decorating and furniture solutions; tells how to add a window, subtract a wall, or lift a ceiling; helps you evaluate the potential of unfinished space; and shows how to build projects that expand space and storage throughout your home.

Nearly 150 color photographs and dozens of drawings, floor plans, charts, and cutaway views show how other families have conquered inner space—and how you can do the same. There's even a special section of templates in the back of the book to help you plan space-efficient furniture arrangements.

We hope you find *Stretching Living Space* a useful addition to your home library. If you do, you may find other books in the **ALL ABOUT YOUR HOUSE** series equally helpful. This major interdepartmental effort draws on the talents and expertise of more than 30 Better Homes and Gardens® editors, designers, writers, and contributors to explore every important element of a modern-day house. Each volume of this information-packed series focuses on a different aspect of your home. Together, the books will help you come to know your home as you never knew it before, because they tell you, quite literally, all about it.

STRETCHING
LIVING
SPACE

CONTENTS

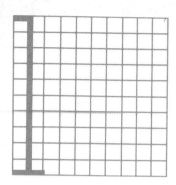

CHAPTER 1

FIRST, SIZE UP YOUR FAMILY'S NEEDS

Perhaps you've said to yourself more than once, "If only this house had another room or a few more closets, I'd really be able to get things organized around here!" Believe it or not, your house may already have that extra needed space; you just have to look for it. It's probably going unused or unnoticed. And if it is, your house isn't working its hardest for you. For example, if your house is average size—say 1,500 square feet—wasting just 10 percent of that space is the same as losing a 10x12-foot room and three closets. Clearly, you can't afford to let areas remain hidden or idle. For general ideas about where to search for more living potential in your house, leaf through this introductory chapter. When you come across an idea that may help solve your problem, turn to the chapter where it's discussed in detail.

DO YOU HAVE ENOUGH EATING SPACE?

Dining is a pleasure best shared with others–but you don't want to literally rub elbows with them. If your family spends more time jockeying for positions at the table than they do enjoying the meal on it, it's time to start looking for more dining room.

But before you start tearing down walls, consider your dining furniture. Would a differently sized or shaped table solve your space problems? The closer the shape of your table matches the shape of the room, the more efficiently you'll use your space. For help in determining the best shape and size dining furniture for your needs, use the furniture templates on pages 152-157, and the planning guidance given in Chapter 3—"Planning Rooms on Paper."

If a simple change in table size or shape won't do the trick, you may have to borrow space from your living room or kitchen. But don't worry about losing space in those rooms. Chapters 2 ("Decorating Strategies To Help Rooms Live Bigger"), 5 ("Structural Surgery"), and 10 ("Space Stretchers You Can Make") show you ways they can lead fuller lives than they now do.

Or maybe you're devoting too much space to a dining room used only a couple of hours a day, or less. Then it's time to make that room work like two (or more) rooms. And Chapter 4 tells all about making a room work double time.

So, if your mealtimes aren't as enjoyable as they could be, seek out the reason why and solve it. Often just one or two changes will turn dining into the pleasurable family experience it should be.

ARE YOU SHORT ON SLEEPING QUARTERS?

Your family's needs change, and bedrooms, because they are the most personal spaces in your house, have to keep up. Older children pursue interests different from those they did in their infant and toddler years, and you may notice that your own needs change, too. If your family is growing, your most obvious need may be for more bedroom space. Expand if you can; but if you just can't, then look for other solutions. In other words, if your family feels a little cramped for space, it may be that your bedrooms are sleeping on the job.

If children are constantly underfoot, maybe they just don't want to play in their rooms. After all, a place with only a bed and bureau isn't much fun. To enliven your children's bedrooms, first try reshuffling furniture. Move the beds into corners; that should free some space for games and toys.

Next, add a few inexpensive and inviting pieces. A couple of bright pillows make excellent inexpensive floor-level seating. For more decorating ideas about making bedrooms more inviting for your children, check out Chapter 2, "Decorating Strategies To Help Rooms Live Bigger."

If two kids who share the same room fight constantly—and you can't give them separate rooms—maybe you need to put them in different corners of the same ring by dividing a single room with a project like the one shown *at left* and *below*. Each side of the divider has space enough to tack up favorite posters and pictures. Each child has a private desk as well. For even more efficient use of bedroom space, these beds fold up and out of the way when playtime rolls around. For more suggestions about making children's rooms more versatile, see Chapter 4, "Doubling Up Lets a Room Do More."

What about your room?

Do you have trouble concentrating on a book because the television is blaring? If so, you need space of your own. A comfortable chair and a good reading lamp will turn your bedroom into a private study. For a closer look at how your bedroom can do double duty, see pages 64 and 65.

Maybe your bedrooms are doing their best now, and still your family needs more sleeping quarters. If you can't afford to move or add on, check for wasted space in your home. When you find it, put it to use. Subdivide a too-big bedroom so one becomes two. Or look for space in a walk-out basement, an underused attic, or part of an attached garage. For a full discussion of each of these last three options, see Chapter 6, "Converting Unfinished Areas."

Finally, don't overlook the possibility of turning closets and storage areas into living space. Page 67 shows how to make a large closet do more than just store. Remember, when it comes to stretching living space in your house, first stretch your imagination.

DOES YOUR FAMILY HAVE A PLACE TO RELAX?

Every family needs a special place where members can all kick off their shoes, stretch out, and take it easy. A relaxing family room can turn even rainy weekends into rewarding and fun times, with all the family gathered to share interests and experiences. Here's how to assess the sociability of your family room. And if your home doesn't even have one, read on.

Most family rooms fall into one of two categories: too big or too small. How can a family room be too big, you ask? The usual clue is that activity areas are tucked into corners, leaving most of the floor area vacant. It's hard to relax and enjoy a room when you have to rearrange its furniture every time someone wants to play a board game or friends drop by for coffee.

Actually, the problem usually lies not with the amount of space but with the way it's used. In Chapter 2, "Decorating Strategies To Help Rooms Live Bigger," you'll see how to subdivide a large family room into more manageable—and functional—living areas. You may gain more room for both personal and family activities and find your family getting together more often.

Stretching family-room space

You know a family room is too small when it begins to look more like a closet than a living space. Out-of-season sports equipment and bundles of newspapers or magazines begin piling up. Chapter 5, "Structural Surgery," shows you how to enlarge a too-tiny room. Here you'll find out that expanding a room is less difficult than you might think. Taking down a wall can turn two small rooms into one large, active living space.

Chapter 5 also shows how to bring more light into a room. Even small spaces become much more livable when you see them in a new light.

Creating a family room

Far worse than a small family room is no family room at all. A home isn't really complete without one. At best, a living room is only a partial substitute because furnishings and flooring here usually are too delicate to take the abuse of constant hard activity. Instead, you want rugged furnishings, such as the economical knockdown seating and storage shown *opposite*. A tile or vinyl floor or tough indoor-outdoor carpet further toughens up a room and makes it easier to clean.

If you have no place other than the living room to serve as a family area, then think the unthinkable: do away with your living room altogether, and convert it into a full-time family room. To save your back and let you know what additional furniture you'll need, Chapter 3, "Planning Rooms on Paper," shows how to visualize possible layouts on graph-paper plans.

Or consider turning an unfinished area into a family space. See Chapter 6, "Converting Unfinished Areas," for this. Or, maybe you can best incorporate a family room by reshuffling your entire house. Check Chapter 8 for advice on starting fresh with a whole-house remodeling.

FIRST, SIZE UP YOUR FAMILY'S NEEDS

HOW DO YOU ENTERTAIN?

Are you more likely to host a black-tie dinner party or a backyard barbecue? Your answer goes a long way toward defining your needs for entertainment space at home. If you answered "both," you had better ask yourself whether your home really can handle each affair equally well. And while you are considering your home's entertainment potential remember to include children's get-togethers. Kids like to play host, too.

For a party to succeed, it needs good conversation and fine food and drink. If your house can't make room for them, then your entertaining will be strained.

A successful party begins at the front door with the way you and your home greet guests. You want to evoke a cordial feeling from the moment they enter. If your entry opens into the middle of the living room, consider adding a small vestibule or greeting area.

Enclosing a porch (see Chapter 7, " Pushing Out") offers one way to do this. A less expensive method is to subdivide your living room so it can handle greeting chores (see Chapter 10, "Space Stretchers You Can Make," for dividers that can help create an entry).

Where will the food go?
Regardless of whether you prefer simple buffets or formal sit-down dinners, your home also must have a comfortable place to serve food. All you really need is a simple table like the one shown here. A photomural behind it lends high-rise elegance to a simple garden apartment. Chapter 4 covers other furnishings that swiftly transform a dining room into an entertainment center.

Finally, a successful party depends on maintaining comfortable social distances between people. A typical conversation circle measures only about 6 feet across for people standing, so you don't need a great deal of space. Just allow enough room for guests to move without constantly bumping into others. (Chapter 3 tells more about creating rooms where people feel at ease.)

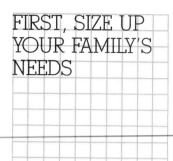

FIRST, SIZE UP YOUR FAMILY'S NEEDS

HOW DO YOU ACCOMMODATE OVERNIGHT GUESTS?

Few modern homes have a "spare room" that's used only when visitors come to town. If your house does, fine. If not—and your guests find themselves camping on a living room sofa bed—consider how space-stretching alternatives could make their stays more comfortable. First let's look at the requirements for any guest sleeping space, then we'll examine ways you can squeeze in overnighters without crowding the family.

A "guest room" begins, of course, with a good bed, preferably one that will slip out of sight when unused. Beds hide away in some surprising packages these days. Pages 68-71 tell about the options available in multipurpose furniture and how you can choose a piece that will assure your visitors a good night's sleep.

Next in importance is privacy. Try to locate guest quarters away from main activity areas —in your home's regular sleeping zone, if possible. Chapter 3, "Planning Rooms on Paper," shows how to analyze your home's layout for maximum efficiency.

No one likes to grope all the way through a darkened, unfamiliar house to get to the bathroom, so quarter visitors handy to one. And consider including linen storage nearby. Guests can help themselves to extra blankets or towels, and you can set up their billet with scarcely an interruption in the conversation. Chapter 10, "Space Stretchers You Can Make," presents ideas for guest linen storage.

Planning for double duty
The best dual-use rooms work equally well in either mode. The family room shown *opposite*, for example, functions for fun, and even includes a wet bar. When the party's over, the owners simply roll up a wood screen and flip down a pair of bunk beds. The wet bar then becomes a vanity for washing up. Storage underneath holds towels and bed linens, as well as the liquor supply.

Folded against the wall, the bunks measure only about 13 inches deep, which means you could easily include a similar setup in a 7-foot-wide closet. An old-fashioned Murphy bed fits into an even narrower closet, or stands up against a wall with storage on either side.

If you have a large room, claim a piece of it for guest sleeping. A single bed, for instance, can fit into a space as small as 6½ x 5 feet; a double needs just 6½ x 6½ feet. Screen off the sleeping nook with a temporary or built-in divider. For more ideas about subdividing a larger room, see pages 40 and 41.

Children's guests
"Overnights" are special occasions for kids, and most like to put up their pals in their rooms. Here all you need is an extra bed, maybe one that can also be used for extra seating. If space is tight, consider constructing a plywood platform with an inexpensive foam mattress and casters so it can roll trundle-style under an ordinary bed.

Adding an extra berth to a child's room offers a way to accommodate adult guests, too. When Grandma visits, one kid can bunk with another, freeing up a room for her use.

When the living room is your only choice
If, in final analysis, your living room offers the only space you have to spare for guest sleeping, don't despair. You can still make it a private, restful place to stay. Allow at least 4 feet of clearance in front of a foldout bed, or place lightweight furnishings there so you can easily open and close the unit. Keep a folding screen and linens close by and you'll be ready to offer hospitality at a moment's notice.

FIRST, SIZE UP YOUR FAMILY'S NEEDS

HOW OLD ARE YOUR CHILDREN?

Children grow not just physically, but intellectually, socially, and emotionally as well. As a parent, your challenge is to develop spaces that stretch along with the kids. Think about the main stages in a child's development—from infancy through the teenage years—and you can anticipate changing needs for your children's personal environments.

Very young children—through toddlers at least—require plenty of contact with adults at all hours of day and night. So you can keep in close touch, locate a nursery convenient to both main living areas and your bedroom. You might even consider temporarily partitioning off a portion of your room.

As children become more mobile, they begin to investigate their environments. Provide them with soft, inviting play surfaces, room for a table or desk, and some storage. Since furnishings and storage should be sized to suit the child, the room needn't be large, but it should be within hailing distance of adult quarters or older children.

Later on
Early in grade school kids begin to wage an on-again-off-again war for independence—at some times they can't get enough of your attention, at others they're preoccupied with their own special pursuits. At this point you might want to consider creating a flexible, farther-away environment like the boys' attic retreat shown here. Ideal for models and telescopes right now, it'll serve just as well for teen activities in a few years. (For two more views of this space, turn to page 100.)

Speaking of teens, they're notoriously demanding of "leave-me-alone" space. And after you've suffered through a boisterous gathering or two, you may be inclined to grant it—even to the extent of a separate suite with its own bath and an outside entrance.

The possibilities for children's space are as varied as children themselves, so keep your mind open for ways to stretch a room's options as you page through this book.

WHAT'S GOING ON IN THE BASEMENT?

Have you taken a look at your basement lately? A really close look? If not, you may discover that it's become little more than a giant closet. Wide-open space down there makes it too easy to hoard junk you would have thrown away years ago if you had no basement. So look again. Basements —along with attics and attached garages— can offer a wealth of potential living space.

Typically dark, poorly ventilated, and repositories for nothing more essential than old snow tires, full basements are blessings often well disguised. If your basement fits this description begin to assess its potential by clearing away as much of the junk as possible. Throw out or give away what you don't need or want. Move the rest into a corner or the furnace room. What remains is space, perhaps more than you had realized. And empty space is the raw material for creating new living areas.

What shape is your basement in?

Now set up a few strong lights and analyze your basement's condition. Are the walls and floor in good shape, without large cracks or crumbling masonry? Is excessive dampness or occasional flooding a problem? If your basement suffers from any of these problems, you'll have to remedy them before starting any finishing project. You can make minor repairs yourself; for major problems, such as flooding, call in an expert. If surfaces are just slightly damp, see page 92 for remedies.

If lots of pipes and ducts jut below the ceiling joists you may have trouble installing an attractive finished ceiling, but you might be able to work around them. For example, in the basement study *at left* the owners left those drainpipes over the desk exposed. Painted a bright color, the pipes become decorative sculpture.

Check local building codes

Now's also the time to investigate your community's building codes. Many prohibit using basements for certain purposes, particularly as bedrooms. (Fire codes usually require two exits—windows included—for every bedroom.) But you shouldn't have any code problem with converting part of your basement into a family room or study.

If your new basement living space will see a lot of come-and-go traffic, check out the stairs. For safety's sake, treads should be at least 9 inches deep; risers no more than 8½ inches high. The stairs need ample lighting at the top and bottom, and should have at least 6½ feet of headroom. if your basement stairs don't measure up now, consider replacing them.

Light up your basement's life

Without a doubt, adequate lighting constitutes the single most important element of a basement conversion, particularly if natural light is scarce or unavailable. Bright, cheerful lighting helps you forget that you're down in the basement. Another way to brighten a basement is to paint the walls and ceilings a light color. Besides spreading illumination, light colors will make a space seem larger than it actually is.

If your basement seems too small for conversion, remember that even a tiny partial basement can hold a crafts center, a darkroom, a sewing niche, a playroom, a study, or a home office—just about any small specialty room. For more about finishing basements, refer to Chapter 6, "Converting Unfinished Areas."

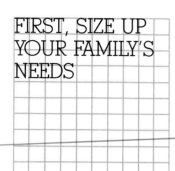

FIRST, SIZE UP YOUR FAMILY'S NEEDS

DO YOU PLAN TO MOVE SOON?

Where will your family be a year or two from now? If the answer is "somewhere else," be sure to exercise special care in planning how you stretch living space. Remodel extensively, and you may not get back your investment when it comes time to sell. Instead, consider inexpensive or portable solutions to make your home more livable. On the other hand, if you don't see a move in the near future—and are tempted to invest in a major remodeling— check pages 138 and 139 to learn which improvements net the best return when you do sell.

The way a home looks plays a big role in the way it lives, so first give thought to what decorating could do for the space situation at your house. Color offers one quick means to visually expand a room. Rearranging the furniture you already have is another. A few pieces of new, compact furniture can add extra function; so can removing items that do little more than clutter a room.

Other ways to help a space look larger include effective use of lighting and mirrors, and putting unused corners and niches to work. And, if you simply don't have enough storage, by all means add portable units you can take with you. All of these ploys, and more, appear in Chapter 2, "Decorating Strategies To Help Rooms Live Bigger."

Remodel if you must

If your family just can't survive comfortably in your house as is, remodeling may be the only way to go. Just bear in mind that even a small-scale remodeling calls for careful planning. You'll want the job to have a professionally finished look, or the results could hurt the market value of your home. For guidance about planning improvements, see chapters 5 ("Structural Surgery"), 6 ("Converting Unfinished Areas"), and 7 ("Pushing Out").

Smaller, less expensive changes can help your house live bigger, too—such as the simple projects detailed in Chapter 10, "Space Stretchers You Can Make." Solve your storage crunch, and many of your other space problems will disappear. You might even decide that you don't need a bigger house after all. And that could save you a bundle.

FIRST, SIZE UP YOUR FAMILY'S NEEDS

WHERE DO YOU DO DESK WORK?

Paying bills is traumatic enough without kids underfoot and a blaring TV—so treat yourself to a special spot for taking care of family business. Children also have important business; they need quiet places to do homework or study for exams. And where does the family chef plan meals and shopping forays? Look for the quiet spots around your home, and put your desks there. Everyone can do better work, in less time, in the right environment.

Start your quest for quiet in your home's sleeping zones. Isolated from through traffic, bedrooms offer get-away-from-it-all privacy, and even small ones usually have enough space for the essentials—a desk, a few shelves, and a lamp (see pages 58 and 59 for a really efficient bedroom office). A window near, but not directly behind, the desk cuts glare and reduces eyestrain.

Guest rooms also make quick studies. All you need are a few simple, inexpensive furnishings. The photo *at right* illustrates how low-cost wire shelving and a plank-top desk can create an efficient, compact see-through work center. Here a studio couch opens up for guests.

For a kitchen planning center you need a surface about 2 feet square with storage for cook books and recipe files. A section of counter works fine, but it should be at desk-top level—about 30 inches. Include a telephone, intercom, and bulletin or blackboard, and your kitchen planning center can become a household command post.

Or look to out-of-the-way, now-unused places. Page 42 shows a desk built for two that wraps around a wasted corner. If all else fails, consider turning a medium- or large-size closet into a mini-study (see Chapter 4, "Doubling Up Lets a Room Do More," for an example of a successful closet conversion). With a closet you can close the door on the clutter of a half-finished project.

COULD A STRETCH SHRINK YOUR ENERGY BILL?

If your house is really cramped, perhaps you've been thinking that just a small addition could make a big difference. Enclosing a porch or bumping out with a mini-addition not only could gain more living space, but also could help keep energy bills down. How? With a sunspace, which is nothing more than a well-insulated room that has large, south-facing windows. Properly designed, a sunspace can provide most of its own heat all winter; some can even help warm the rest of your home. You might get a bonus of fresh vegetables during the cold months, too. Here are the main ingredients of a successful sunspace.

A well-designed sunspace has three elements: collectors, heat storage, and a control system. Look at the garden room shown here to see how each works. The most common *collectors* are normal double- or triple-pane windows. Ideally these should be angled to maximize solar heat gain, as shown *above*. For *heat storage* good sunspaces use masonry floors or tanks of liquid to soak up the day's solar harvest, then radiate it back into living quarters after sundown.

Finally, your room needs a system of *controls* to move heat where you need it—and keep it there. Doors and vents between the sun-room and other spaces do the first job; insulation in the walls and over the glass at night handles the second. Here, for example, a roll-down exterior canvas shade helps hold heat at night and can aid in keeping out searing summer sun. Overhangs and awnings also can serve as sun control devices.

To work together, these elements need careful designing. That's why it's so important to work with a professional builder or architect who has had experience in solar design. Insist on visiting previous jobs, preferably ones that have experienced at least one winter and summer.

Interested in adding a sunspace to your house? Chapter 7, "Pushing Out," surveys your options.

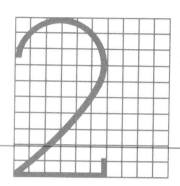

DECORATING STRATEGIES TO HELP ROOMS LIVE BIGGER

Have you ever been amazed by a photograph or painting you could swear was three-dimensional? If so, you already know that spaciousness is largely in the eye of the beholder. This chapter introduces you to color, scale, mirrors, lighting, and other decorating devices that visually can stretch a room well beyond its physical dimensions. Of course rooms are for living in as well as looking at, so we have also included information about practicalities such as how to arrange furniture and where to "find" wasted space, along with dozens of storage possibilities you may have overlooked.

Used adeptly, color can make a small room seem bigger or a big one smaller, elongate a boxy space or square up a long and narrow one, bring down a too-high ceiling, or raise one that's visually too low for comfort.

The key to pulling off any of these tricks is to understand how color works. Light or low-key colors *reflect* light, making them seem to recede from your field of vision. Use them to push a wall, ceiling, or floor away from you and create an illusion of greater space.

Conversely, dark hues *absorb* light and seem to advance toward you. Contrasted with light tones, dark colors can pull in a distant wall or other faraway surface, giving a room more pleasing proportions than it had before.

Color out flaws

Color can also mask architectural shortcomings. Paint or paper an awkwardly placed door to match the walls, and the door virtually disappears.

In fact, coloring out distracting elements of any sort—good or bad—helps a room live bigger. The greater an unbroken expanse of pale or cool color, the stronger the sense of space.

In the room shown *at right*, for example, a pale, neutral scheme unifies everything—walls, ceiling, window treatments, furnishings, and floor—for a space that feels far more expansive than its 15x18-foot dimensions. All those neutrals could make a room bland, but not here, thanks to a rich mix of contrasting textures.

CHANGE THE VERTICAL DIMENSION

High ceilings and graciously proportioned rooms seem to have become true relics. If you are lucky enough to have a grand old house —or a cathedral ceiling in a newer one—by all means play up its architectural assets. If you are not so fortunate, here are some fool-the-eye formulas that can visually lift your ceilings.

We've seen on the preceding pages how a light color on the ceilings and walls seems to increase a room's height, and also expand the room as a whole. Now let's look at some other approaches that can achieve the same effect.

Bold verticals
Just as vertical lines in clothing seem to increase a person's height, vertical lines in a room "raise" the ceiling. A tall piece of furniture, for instance, or floor-to-ceiling shelving with strong vertical supports, has a room-heightening effect. So does a bold, vertically striped wall covering or a large piece of art that is considerably taller than it is wide.

Architectural ploys can play up the vertical, too. Consider installing floor-to-ceiling beams at intervals along walls or at windows. Few windows stretch the full height of a room, but you can make them seem to do so with shutters or mini-slat blinds. In the room pictured *at near right*, eight louvered panels give the ceiling a boost, and also screen out an awkward window.

Lead the eye upward
Another effective way to alter a room's vertical dimensions is to create interest high on the wall. Some examples:
• Place a brass planter or basket with dried flowers on top of an already-tall armoire or breakfront.
• Install a shelf over a high window and display a miscellany of collectibles such as

antique toys, old books, straw flowers, and crockery.
• Make a towering palm or other indoor tree a key element in your room's scheme.
• Emphasize near-the-ceiling interest with strategically placed track spotlighting. (More about the tricks you can play with lighting on pages 38 and 39.)
• To dramatize a cathedral ceiling, break the usual rules and hang an art arrangement high on the wall.

• On high Victorian ceilings or others trimmed with decorative moldings, draw the eye upward with stripes of color on the moldings.

Pulling it all together
Of course you can work any combination of these strategies. In the sitting room shown *opposite*, for example, white— lavished over walls, woodwork, moldings, the already-high ceiling, and chairs and sofa— gives a quietly soaring effect. In contrast, a sweep of bold color in an abstract painting hangs purposely above eye level to draw attention upward.

SCALE FURNITURE TO SUIT THE SPACE

Successful decorating in a pocket-size space depends on properly scaled furnishings. As you may know, any piece of furniture and any accessory have two weights—real and visual. To open up a room, select furnishings that *appear* to be light in weight. Glass-top tables, a sofa that seems to float on a recessed base, pieces with clean and simple lines, open-arm chairs that allow you to see beyond to what surrounds them—all are good examples of what to look for when you are scaling furniture to a small room.

Scale is the relationship between an object and its surrounding space; this means that visual size is even more important than actual dimensions. The more closely upholstery fabrics and window treatments blend with their backgrounds, the less they seem to "weigh" visually. And tables and chests with shiny or reflective surfaces seem less bulky than heavily textured ones. Open storage—a baker's rack, for example—is much lighter in scale than an enclosed wood piece of the same size.

Your furnishings should also be in proportion both to the size of the room and to one another, with a good balance of size and form, and color, pattern, and texture.

Focus on a focal point

To make a room work, you must establish a center of interest, or a focal point. It might be an existing architectural feature such as a fireplace, a large piece of furniture, or a painting. Group the room's furnishings about this focal point or visual anchor. A pair of chairs and an end table will balance a love seat or sofa; even some oversized furniture will work as long as surfaces are reflective but low-keyed, and blend with their surroundings.

In the tiny living room *at left,* a pair of love seats placed face to face establish the focal conversation area. A pair of chrome-and-cane armchairs from the dining area add seating but take up little visual or actual space. A clear acrylic cocktail table provides for snacks, yet in itself practically disappears, as do the four chrome pharmacy lamps supported on acrylic standards.

31

PARE DOWN FURNISHINGS

When a room seems cramped, take a good look at what you have —and what you could live without. Reduce your furnishings to essentials. Use multipurpose furniture for most efficiency. Strive for a clutter-free environment. Keep windows and floors simple. Clear-the-deck decorating not only helps rooms to live bigger, it also eases their day-to-day living and maintenance.

Probably the least expensive way to ease the space squeeze is to put your rooms on a diet. All too often our homes look as if pack rats live there. Begin by stripping away the nonessentials in a room. Banish some pieces to other rooms, other pieces to storage, still others to thrift shops or friends. Strive for an absolute absence of clutter. In so doing, you'll simplify your life as well as your decorating scheme.

Don't think for a moment we're suggesting you divest yourself of your most prized possessions. Instead, select a few that will create the best visual effect for the particular place and occasion. Store others that you really want to keep; these you can bring out another time and rotate with current ones for a change of mood and pace.

Simplifying window and floor treatments
The more you make windows fade into the background, the more opened-up a room will feel. Rule out frilly curtains and heavy draperies in favor of more streamlined solutions. With proper treatment, you can remedy even disturbing proportions or placement of a window. Both mini-slat blinds and vertical blinds are masters of disguise and spare in look. Louvered shutters and Roman shades offer two additional popular pared-down looks. And, of course, totally undraped windows are the most stripped-down of all.

As for floors, nothing is quite so pared down as a polished wood floor left bare—unless

it's a bleached or painted floor also left bare. Wall-to-wall carpet will have a similar, but warmer, effect.

Take advantage of multipurpose furniture
To help reduce furnishings, press multi-function pieces into service wherever possible. Why devote space and money to two pieces when one piece can do more than one job just as well? A wicker trunk serves end-table duty, and provides storage, too. An upholstered bed strewn with plump pillows stands in for a sofa. Built-ins take up precious little floor space yet serve for both storage and display. (More about multipurpose furniture on pages 68-71.)

The room shown *at right* makes the most of the minimal concept, and also demonstrates many of the paring-down ideas we've just discussed. Instead of a sofa, a bay window is cushioned for seating. Four large floor pillows covered to match sit lightly on a natural sisal rug "island." A sanded and finished wooden skid from a warehouse has become a low-profile cocktail table.

Pared down doesn't mean naked, however. Here trim built-ins disguise a radiator on one side, storage on the other, and stereo speakers above. A pair of large, dried bouquets in the niches soars dramatically above the built-ins, proving that two large pieces can generate a much greater effect than would a miscellany of smaller, less impressive ones.

TRY A NEW ARRANGEMENT

In one respect, space is a bit like money—it's not the amount you have, but how you use it that counts. Often just pushing your present furniture into a different relationship gives both the furnishings and the room new life.

Furniture that just lines up against walls, dancing-school style, usually makes a room seem awkward and static. Choreograph those wallflowers with an unorthodox arrangement and you will turn an ordinary, almost dead room into an extraordinarily alive one—and the room will function better, too.

One big reason up-against-the-wall arrangements nearly always turn out to be dull is that window and door openings severely limit a room's possibilities. You get to thinking the sofa *has* to go in a certain spot; then chairs, table, and other pieces just "naturally" fall into highly predictable, indeed inevitable, places.

Begin thinking about how your furniture might be rearranged by imagining the room totally empty. This does not mean you have to move everything out. Instead, draw the room to scale, as explained in Chapter 3 (pages 46 and 47). Next, make cutouts of the furniture you now own—or would like to buy—and move them around on your plan. This experimentation in itself, even if your mind starts "blank," will begin to generate new, fresh ideas. (Templates in the back of this book—on pages 152-157—show the shapes and sizes for most major pieces of furniture.)

Try a new slant

As you experiment with away-from-the-walls arrangements, realize that now furniture needn't even be parallel to a

room's boundaries. Freed from the walls, a diagonal layout animates a room, and works especially well in rooms broken up by numerous windows and doors.

Consider, too, how an island arrangement can divide a room's functions. Here are some examples:

• Instead of lining low storage units for stereo, records, and books along a wall, arrange them back-to-back with a sofa out in the room; the surface of the units then doubles as a sofa table for a lamp and for reading material.

• "Float" a bed in the middle of the room, perhaps with storage modules lined up at both head and foot.

• Even a traditional conversation grouping takes on a fresh new look when pulled into the center of the room and anchored with an area rug.

The grouping shown *opposite* exemplifies what can happen when furniture moves away from the walls. The pair of sofas sit face to face and perpendicular to a fireplace wall. A sisal rug anchors the conversation area. An ottoman and cube, angled to line up with diagonal flooring, add visual interest to a space otherwise dominated by squares and parallels.

Modulars on the move
Somewhat of a newcomer to the furniture scene are modular seating pieces, which allow unprecedented flexibility in

room arranging. Why, after all, does furniture have to be rooted to one spot? Corner, armless, and ottoman modules become an L-shape sectional one day, a pair of love seats and chaise the next. Depending on the pieces you choose, the combinations for saving space and changing the scene are myriad.

Modular storage can also do wonders for a room arrangement. In the bedroom shown *below,* vertical storage units free floor space that would be

taken up with a conventional dresser and chest of drawers. Previously wasted vertical space stores everything from clothing and stereo gear to kids' toys, and a window turns into a headboard wall. The saved floor space frees room for a lounge chair and a slatted bench, which also triples as step stool, bench, and television table.

Imaginative options
Although one arrangement may seem to work best in a

given room for now, you're likely to discover several equally interesting options for the same furniture you can draw on for future layouts. So get out ruler, tracing paper, and scissors, and put your imagination to work. Whatever arrangement or rearrangement you are planning, keep traffic patterns in mind; that is, always be sure that your furniture's layout aids, not impedes, movement into, through, or out of the room. (More about traffic patterns in Chapter 3.)

CREATE ILLUSIONS WITH MIRRORS

Want a nearly foolproof way to make rooms seem wider, longer, or brighter? Install a mirror and you instantly double your visual living space. Mirrors can do a lot more, too. Gang a group of them in strips, squares, or circles; position one mirror to catch the reflection from another; create further interest by placing one or two mirrors at an unusual angle or in an unexpected location.

Think of any mirror as a magic window that teases you into seeing beyond or through a solid surface. In the minuscule sitting room pictured *opposite*, for instance, a trio of smoked panels makes a corner conversation grouping look like a much more expansive island arrangement.

First let's consider some of the many ways mirrors might open up areas in your home. Then we'll list some other special effects you can achieve.
• A mirror strategically placed to reflect the outdoors will appear as another window.
• Mirroring the long wall of a narrow room makes the room immediately appear wider.
• Mirroring an awkwardly placed column, corner, or beam can make it do a disappearing act.
• A fireplace mirrored above and along its sides seemingly will "float" in space.
• A large, mirror-top table adds dazzle yet loses visual weight.
• A mirrored screen reflects in more than one direction, adding multiple dimensions.
• A mirror on the back wall of a display case doubles the size of the collection.
• Mirrors between kitchen counter and wall cabinets open up closed space in a small kitchen.
• Mirroring bedroom closet doors enlarges space, and adds obvious practicality.
• Mirrors in the bathroom let you see yourself in three dimensions when you have a pair that adjust for back-of-the-head viewing. And don't overlook mirroring the back of a door here, too.

Reflections in pieces

A new entry on the market is the mirror strip. Available in a variety of lengths and widths, strips are easy to handle, cutting down on the high cost of labor for installation. Furthermore, you can achieve the same expansive effects with lots less mirror simply by placing strips at intervals as opposed to covering the entire space. And like many plate mirrors, strips are available in mood-making tones such as bronze and smoke.

Another way to achieve a dramatic effect is to line up a row of inexpensive circles of mirror on a wall, or place them at random.

In the entry hall *above*, identical mirrors line up like portholes, not only opening up a narrow space, but adding a touch of whimsy as well.

For do-it-yourselfers, there's the ubiquitous mirror tile—a 12-inch square with a self-stick back that's a cinch to install on walls, beams, furniture, any place you'd like to add dazzle. Mirror tiles go virtually any place a standard plate mirror goes, and beyond. Use tiles to cover a headboard, to stripe a small hall, to face a fireplace, or to line closet doors. You will find the possibilities are almost infinite.

DRAMATIZE
WITH LIGHT

As a cosmetic is to a face, lighting is to a home's interior. Effectively used, light beautifies and creates moods that bring out a room's best. Light can make a small area look suddenly spacious, accentuate a room's assets, minimize its flaws, or fill empty corners. A few of these light touches can change a room from dull to spectacular.

All too often lighting in a room consists of nothing more than a boring band of eye-level illumination. Position accent lights above or below this band and you can create some far more interesting effects.

To discover how, experiment at night with a couple of inexpensive clamp lights. Move them around the room, placing them to simulate some of the following:
• Spots and floodlights, either freestanding or fitted into wall- or ceiling-mounted tracks, focus a strong beam on a single object, or cause a wall seemingly to recede by bathing all or most of it in light.
• Canister up-lights placed on the floor can footlight a sculpture or large plant, cast playful patterns of light and shadow, or bring a corner to life.
• Recessed lighting, placed strategically beneath a platform

bed, at the sides of stairs, or above glass shelving, expands space by giving objects the impression of floating.
• In almost any lamp or fixture, smoked, bronzed, or colored bulbs create mood.
• Easy-to-install dimmer switches give you the option of controlling light from subtle to bright, further regulating the mood and establishing spatial illusion.

The small room *opposite* takes on sumptuous proportions thanks to a carefully calculated combination of light sources. A pharmacy floor lamp provides task light for reading. A simple canister

up-light casts fused strips of light and shadow in a once-dark corner filled with plants. Low-voltage pin spots and a framing projector with a perforated filter are mounted on a single ceiling track; they throw additional light patterns on the wall and focus light on special objects throughout the room.

In the room shown *above left,* track lighting with color filters, adjustable louvers, and focusing lenses washes one wall with a mood-enhancing glow, "frames" a picture, and highlights a mobile cocktail table below.

Neon art mounted on a mirrored ceiling, *above right,* opens up a tiny entryway. Simple spots illuminate paintings on the wall beyond, giving warm, inviting indirect lighting.

DECORATING STRATEGIES TO HELP ROOMS LIVE BIGGER

SUBDIVIDE SPACES

To heighten the livability of a small space, treat it as more than one room. When you subdivide a space to serve multiple functions, it lives bigger instantly. You can achieve subdividing either physically (with screens, dividers, and plants) or visually (with area rugs and differing color schemes).

Screens are a wonderfully mobile solution to sectioning a room—either alone, or with other freestanding furniture pieces such as a sofa, bookcase, or buffet. Placed strategically, any of these creates an entryway where none exists, defines a dining area in one end of a living room, partitions off a sitting area in a bedroom, or a home office in a family room.

An airy, see-through option is a "wall" of living plants; this is especially effective when you need to define a nonexistent foyer, dining room, or other space where an open feeling is paramount.

To create a living wall, begin with an assortment of plants of different heights. Place them on the floor in a waterproof pan, pebble-lined for drainage. Then suspend hanging plants at different heights from the ceiling above. The result: an indoor garden that divides and delights.

On wall-to-wall carpet or on bare wood, area rugs are great unifiers. More than one in a room can create islands of function, direct traffic flow, and increase living space by separating activities.

The living room *at right*, for example, functions as if it were three rooms in one: one area rug defines a cozy fireside setting; a matching rug anchors an intimate conversation grouping, and sets off a grand piano beyond.

Another way to divide a room visually is to break it up with two or more related patterns or color schemes. Painting or papering the walls of a corner or alcove in contrast to—but coordinated with—the rest of the room will set it visibly apart.

PUT CORNERS AND ODD SPACES TO WORK

Corners, leftovers such as the slivers of space behind an open door, the cubby beneath a stairway, the back of a closet—you can probably find an under-used nook or cranny in almost every room in your house. Here are some ideas to help you put these usable areas to work.

Corners are extra-special spaces, and rate extra-special treatment. Use a corner to create a focal point with plants, art, or a treasured antique. Fit another corner with seating. Camouflage storage behind a handsome corner screen. Build in a china cabinet. What you do with a corner depends partly on what you need, and partly on what the corner itself has to offer.

In the upstairs room shown *above,* an under-the-eaves outside corner didn't at first seem to have much going for it. Low knee walls limited headroom,

and a bed or beds here would have taken up too much floor space. The solution: a wrap-around study center for two. Open and simple construction puts the sizable desk, which is topped with reflective glass, into scale with its surroundings; vertically striped wallpaper helps lift the ceiling.

If you decide to line a corner with seating, consider a pair of built-in banquettes such as those shown *opposite.* Slim

upholstered benches have been hugging restaurant walls for years, and they make just as much sense in any tight corner. These consist of plywood bases topped with foam, covered with shirred fabric, and garnished with a profusion of throw pillows. Space-thrifty wall lamps eliminate any need for end tables.

Behind open doors, under stairways

If you have a door that normally stands ajar, look behind it and you'll probably find a sliver of space—6 inches or so deep—that could take on new purpose. Bookshelves sized especially for paperbacks fit neatly back here, as do a row or several rows of coat hooks. Behind-the-door space that's just a little deeper might be ideal for that much-needed pantry or broom closet.

If space under a stairway isn't already in use—for a closet, powder room, or other stairs—by all means press it into service. This might be just the place for your stereo gear; add storage for a projector and screen, and your video equipment, and you'll have a complete home entertainment center.

Fitted with a desk and shelving, under-stair space can also serve as a home office, one that can be closed off with doors, if you like. (Pages 62 and 63 show yet another use for space beneath stairs.)

Under windows, in kitchens
Dormer, bay, and corner windows also offer developable space. Here you can usually count on light and a view, so consider a big planter or cozy window seat. In a dining room or alcove, you might want to use under-window space for a serving shelf.

Need a breakfast place, extra counter space, or a desk for household paperwork? Even the smallest corner or alcove in a kitchen could yield an answer.

A triangular counter and two bar stools could provide eating and counter space; if you added shelving, you could do desk work here, too.

CUT CLUTTER
WITH STORAGE

Clear away clutter and you instantly open up a room. But where's all that clutter going to go? Organization is the key. Couple it with ingenuity —that elusive ability that allows you to see beyond the obvious stashing spaces to more creative solutions—and you'll find relief for overstuffed rooms.

In making room for storage, the challenge lies not so much in finding more space as in making better use of space that already exists. For example, once-unused attic space, *below,* has been turned into storage, plus a sewing center. When not in use, the flip-down table becomes a door that neatly hides the sewing machine and supplies.

Use vertical space
To free floor space, put walls to work. An obvious storage solution is the use of wall-climbing furniture such as breakfronts and bookcases, highboys and armoires. Similarly, built-ins can go floor to ceiling to house possessions— either behind closed doors or on open display.

Organized storage is the key to tidiness in the teen room, *opposite above.* Nestled under the eaves, a built-in window seat doubles as a bookshelf beneath wall-hung shelves for collectibles. Baskets tucked under the seat provide additional stashing space.

Modular, stackable, and bunchable storage systems offer even more flexibility, allowing you to customize storage for your needs. Also, many are freestanding, so you can create walls of storage where none exists.

Don't overlook up
Often neglected are tops of tall furniture and built-ins. There wicker baskets or terra cotta pots would look spectacular, and you could stow small treasures as well.

Or, you might delegate space above a window or door to storage by installing a shelf. Painted to match the wall, the shelf becomes a barely visible catchall for a conglomeration of things.

Opt for organizers
To help make order out of chaos, look for ready-made organizers (such as those listed below), available at hardware stores, kitchen and closet shops, and department stores:
• Drawer dividers that keep utensils within reach in the kitchen can also organize cosmetics in the bath.
• Extra clothes poles and stackable, modular drawers can practically double the capacity of a closet.
• An under-the-bed box turns once-wasted space into out-of-season clothes storage.
• Perforated hardboard mounted on the wall can organize anything from pots and pans in the kitchen to a collection of hobby and sports gear.

Modular drawers literally furnish a bedroom in storage, *opposite below,* preserving its uncluttered look. The same type of units bunch together to form a bed platform, and stack into a bedside table and a pair of towering chests.

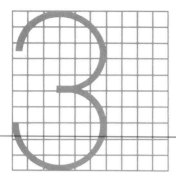

PLANNING ROOMS ON PAPER

If you've ever moved a piano, you can appreciate the convenience of planning room arrangements on paper. Drawing a room to scale, cutting out templates that represent your furniture pieces, and moving the templates around on the plan saves your back—and gives you an opportunity to see the room arranged in a variety of ways. You just study each plan and visualize living with it. Pages 152-157 present a series of furniture templates you can trace, then cut out; this chapter shows how to work with them.

When it comes to furniture juggling, a steel tape, ruler, pencil, and knife can do the work of an entire moving crew. You don't need any special drafting skills, either; the process is only a bit more difficult than playing with paper dolls.

Measuring is the first step, and one of the most critical—so be sure to measure accurately. With a carpenter's rule or steel tape, measure each wall at floor level to prevent sagging that could distort measurements. Record the length of each wall, then measure a second time to double-check your accuracy.

Next, measure the width of each window and door from the outer edges of the frames. Then measure the distances between each door and window and the nearest room corner—or any other architectural feature, such as a fireplace or jog in the wall. (For a fireplace, be sure to record its width and the width and the depth of its hearth.)

The paper plot

With all the dimensions recorded, you're ready to lay out your room on graph paper. Buy ¼-inch graph paper at a stationery or art supply store.

Plot the dimensions of your room on the paper, allowing ¼ inch per foot of wall space. Our inset photo *opposite upper left* shows how to draw open double lines for windows, filled-in double lines for walls, and open spaces for doors. If a door opens into the room, indicate the area of its swing with an arc. This assures that you won't place furniture on a collision course with the door.

Also note on your floor plan all electrical outlets, light switches, radiators, air conditioners, and any other built-in features that might affect furniture layouts.

No-strain furniture moving

Your next step is to bring in the furniture. Start by measuring all the pieces you expect to put in the room, including area rugs.

The templates on pages 152-157 include outlines for most of the typical sizes and styles of furniture. If you don't find a template for an item you have, measure carefully and develop your own. Use dotted lines to indicate door swings and drawer paths with any storage pieces.

The photos *opposite page* show how to develop a plan and cutouts for your room. On upcoming pages we'll show how you can put paper to work dealing with traffic patterns, creating conversation areas, and solving typical plan problems.

The important thing to remember at this stage is that a room can have more than one arrangement. Keep playing with the possibilities until you find the one that works best. Then you'll have to move the furniture only once.

Exercise special care when you're drawing up your graph-paper plan. Miss by just a square and your room will appear a foot bigger or smaller than it actually measures. Count squares along each length and each width, then double-check them by measuring the plan with a ruler. Most interior walls are about 6 inches thick, so al- low a half-square for them. To improve visibility, color tracing paper with a felt tip pen before you trace the shapes; to color-coordinate an arrangement, use felt tip pens in appropriate hues.

For accuracy, use scis- sors or a sharp knife to cut out the templates. A knife also comes in handy for moving the cutouts around on your room plan.

PLANNING ROOMS ON PAPER

MAPPING TRAFFIC LANES

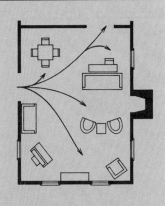

TRAFFIC PATTERNS

Two-door room
Doorways in two adjacent walls virtually amputate one corner of this room. The best solution for situations like this is to use that isolated corner for a furniture grouping that will function independently from the rest of the room. Here, a game table and chairs made sense. A desk, piano, or crafts center would create the same kind of independent arrangement.

The more doors a room has, the more lanes of traffic you have to accommodate. Fail to direct that traffic and you may find yourself caught in a stream of meandering family members whose only way to get through a room is to walk through your conversation. By arranging furniture to create corridors and pathways, you can deflect a stampede of passers-through.

First look at where a room's doors are and how they determine natural traffic paths. Plan a furniture arrangement that encourages this natural flow or that directs it a more advantageous way. Allow at least 2 feet for a lane of traffic.

The process of elimination
Sometimes you can't create the right traffic pattern by just rearranging the furniture you have. Instead you may have to replace some pieces with others that fit the space better. The photos *opposite* and *above* and the floor plans *below* show you how a traffic problem was solved by eliminating some pieces of furniture and acquiring others.

In the "before" photo, *above*, a sofa and love seat are on opposite sides of this small room, forcing traffic through the center of conversation. In the "after" photo, *opposite*, two trim new occasional chairs replace the overscale sofa. The entire grouping is perpendicular to the window wall, which frees up a traffic corridor on the right. A slim new wall unit provides needed storage. The old sofa, rocker, and oversized lounge chair were moved to the den.

Three-door room
Three doorways naturally cut a room into three areas. In the plan shown here, the major furniture grouping consists of a conversation island pulled in away from the two main pathways. The back of the sofa creates one path. In the bay window area, a love seat and table tuck in out of the way of traffic along the second passageway.

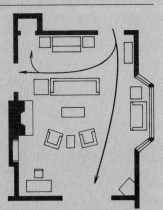

Four-door room
Do you have a room with a doorway in each of its four walls? If so, the best arrangement for this is to channel traffic straight through from the entry door to the doorway opposite. Here a long table and chair define a corridor through the room. Corners and areas of the room that once were cut off by the traffic now play host to small furniture groupings.

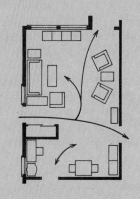

BEFORE

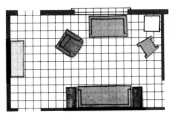

AFTER

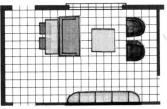

CREATING CONVERSATION AREAS

The art of conversation depends a lot on the furniture grouping in which the conversation takes place. Friendly, animated chat just won't occur when people are scattered to the far ends of the room. So, if you're after relaxed conversation, arrange seating pieces in comfortable groups separated by the right social spaces. And just what are the right dimensions for social spaces? Pull up a chair, and let's talk about it.

It's all but impossible to converse in a room with furniture lined up against the walls as if for a gangland execution. Shouting across an area blasts away any intimacy you might establish.

Instead, seat your family and guests comfortably close and out of the room's main traffic pattern. Understand what makes a conversation area work and you're on your way to some delightful chats.

How many people?
Unless you give lectures in your room, don't plan to seat more than five or six persons in any single conversation area. When more than half a dozen gather, some participants will have to overcome cross talk—or will feel isolated and remain silent.

If your room is very large or you're inclined to entertain large groups, create several conversation pockets. Rather than add to the size of a single conversation area, add more areas to a room.

How large a space?
For easy conversation, arrange your furniture to seat six people with no one farther than 8 feet from anyone else. Ideally, the most distant people should be able to reach out and touch fingertips.

A comfortable conversation area provides table space for snacks, drinks, and ashtrays, so include side tables or a coffee table in your grouping. Allow a minimum of 15 inches legroom between a sofa or chair and your coffee table.

What kind of furniture?
The standard anchor for most furniture groupings is a single sofa or love seat, but you can create a successful arrangement with more than one sofa or with a grouping of chairs. Actually, the furniture itself is less important than where you place it in a room and how well one seating piece relates to others in a grouping.

Scale other furniture essentials to the seating pieces. Side tables should correspond to the height of the seat or arm of the sofa or chair beside them.

Place lamps around a room so their light is equally distributed. Avoid hot spots of concentrated lighting as well as dark holes.

Anchored or floating?
Whether you choose to float an island grouping in open floor space or tie your conversation grouping to a wall depends mainly on the size of the room and its architecture. A large room looks cozier and less ballroom-like if its conversation grouping is out in the center or diagonally across a corner of the room. A small room, especially one with a solid wall away from the main traffic pattern, usually works well with a conversation grouping arranged perpendicular to that wall.

Basic shapes
The opposite page presents eight different ways to group conversation areas. No two are exactly alike—in either arrangement or type of pieces used. Adapt these configurations to your furniture, or think in terms of basic shapes or groupings and go on to create your own arrangement.

• An *L-shape arrangement,* such as plans 1 and 6, offers you two sides of seating with, perhaps, a corner table and a coffee table. Watch that the outside seats don't get too far apart to allow for comfortable conversation.

To expand seating, add a bench, stool, or ottoman as in grouping 6.

• A *U-shape arrangement,* such as plans 7 and 8, or a modified U, such as plan 5, offers an opportunity for the occupants in each corner to converse separately.

• A *parallel arrangement,* such as plans 2 and 3, or a variation of this arrangement, such as plan 4, puts people directly opposite each other, often with a coffee table between the seating pieces.

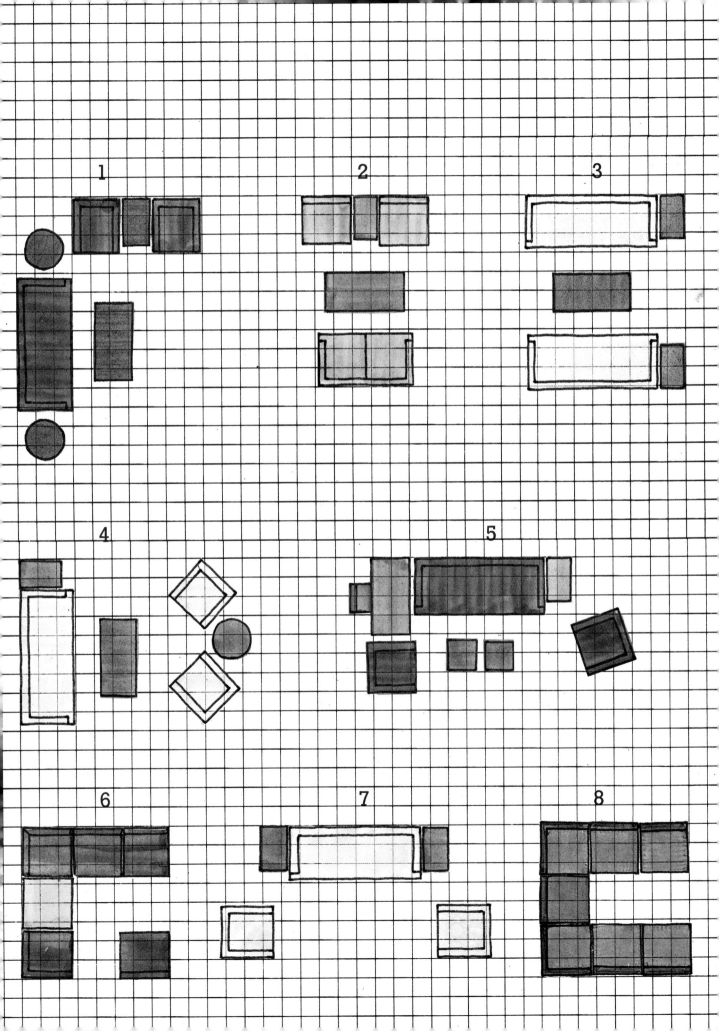

1

2

3

4

5

6

7

8

SOLVING PLAN PROBLEMS: SMALL ROOMS

Having a small room isn't the worst thing that can happen to a person —but not knowing what to do with it is! When space is limited, furniture has to be scaled to the area, chosen in colors that blend into the surroundings without jarring contrast, and —above all—arranged properly. Overload a tiny space with furniture or get lax about an orderly arrangement, and your small room can turn into a big disaster.

If yours is a pocket-size living room, here are some techniques to help it live as big as it possibly can.

• *First:* Limit the furniture you put into it. The 14x14-foot room shown here keeps major items to a spare minimum— just a smooth-lined sofa and a pair of light-scaled, open-arm chairs covered in rust-colored fabric. (Use solids rather than patterns whenever you want a piece to look as small as possible.)

A creamy Oriental rug, two tables, two sleek lamps, and carefully rationed accessories complete the furnishings here. A built-in bookcase saves precious floor space.

• *Second:* Plan for auxiliary seating. When a room is small and it's impractical to add a lot of upholstered pieces, make sure that you have some extra benches, stools, or folding chairs waiting in the wings. For this room, two upholstered benches line the hallway wall, waiting to be called into play.

• *Third:* Decorate with a light touch. Choose open-arm or open-back chairs rather than solid upholstered versions; opt for shelves instead of massive cabinets. A glass- or acrylic-topped table has less visual weight than a wood piece of the same size. Keep your color palette on the light side as well. Cover large upholstered pieces and walls in light colors. Reserve bold shades only for accents.

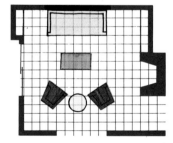

SOLVING PLAN PROBLEMS: BIG SPACES

A large room radiates a sense of magnificence—and if the room also has a lot of windows, so much the better. But big rooms—even medium-size spaces with few uninterrupted walls—pose special planning challenges: how do you maintain comfortable social distances between people, and how do you arrange furniture so it won't block views and ventilation? Here are solutions for both of these problems.

The living room shown *above* and in the plan *at right* measures 18 feet wide by 31 feet long by 9 feet high—noble proportions that would seem cavernous if furnishings weren't selected and arranged with care.

If your home has a room like this, you've probably already noticed how ordinary-scale furniture, spread out in an attempt to fill the space, looks puny and disconnected. To pull together an expansive scene, use a combination of two decorating stratagems.

Furnish large rooms in a big way
Pleasing scale depends on a proper balance between proportions. Big rooms seem more intimate and organized if furniture is sized to its surroundings.

Here a 7-foot-long sofa and two 5-foot love seats fill the space. The effect is a soft, in-

viting look that would be difficult to achieve with a clutter of smaller, more delicately scaled furniture. In the background a grand piano adds more visual heft.

Develop separate areas within a room
Big furniture alone won't tame a large space. You also have to arrange it in groupings scaled to human proportions. Check the plan and you'll see that this rectangular room really is three subdivided areas.

At one end wall, near the door, a pair of chairs flanks a round table. In the center the sofa, love seats, and a big rug define the main conversation area. At the far end the piano, shelving, and a drop-front desk form a library and music center. One of the love seats, placed perpendicular to the sofa wall, divides these last zones.

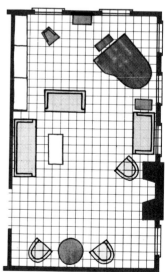

SOLVING PLAN
PROBLEMS:
AWKWARD ROOMS

Sometimes a room can seem to have too many architectural features. Here, for example, awkwardly spaced windows and doors, along with a massive fireplace, cut up every wall. To make matters worse, all of the windows drop to floor level, and a set of French doors draws traffic through the room to a terrace outside. Light and views in three directions certainly make this a cheerful, sunny space, but where do you put the furniture?

Float a grouping

The way out of this planning plight is to pull your furniture away from those chopped-up walls and float a conversation center in the middle of the room. Don't insist on filling every corner; if furniture works

better out in the middle, that's where it should be.

Here a checked sofa faces the ceiling-high fireplace, the room's natural focal point. Matching light-scale occasional chairs and a treasured antique rocker flank the sofa to create a U-shape arrangement. A handsome Chinese area rug anchors the floating grouping.

Rugs also offer a good way to define the boundaries of a floating grouping. Even if your room has wall-to-wall carpet, consider overlaying it with an area rug to make a conversation center especially cushy and inviting. If you're using cutouts and graph paper to

plan a room, experiment with pieces of colored paper until you find the size and shape of rug that will work best.

Floating basics

As you experiment with floating furniture arrangements, keep two points in mind:
• Though the grouping needn't touch any one wall, it must visually connect with a focal point. Here the focal point is a fireplace; at your house it might be a bay window that commands a nice view, a storage wall with an interesting array of books and accessories, or an especially compelling piece of art.
• Pay close attention to traffic patterns. A floating arrangement can improve the traffic flow, or make it worse. In this case the grouping channels traffic behind the sofa, allowing easy access to the French doors and to the opposite end of the room.

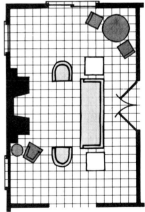

SOLVING PLAN PROBLEMS: TOO MANY WINDOWS AND DOORS

Too much often is as bad as too little. Features normally considered architectural assets—such as windows and focal points—turn into something less than blessings in a space over-endowed with them. The room on this page, for instance, has so many windows the homeowners found themselves arranging furniture in a fishbowl. And the room *opposite* had a split personality, with not one but two logical and very attractive focal points. Here's how to arrange space in rooms that have more than you bargained for.

Windows and doors left only a few linear feet of wall space in the living room/solarium shown *above* and in the plan *at right*. What's more, the two areas, though small separately, together were just a little too big for a unified furniture grouping.

Once again, the solution was to create two separate groupings. In the solarium the owners grouped four lightly scaled chairs around a see-through coffee table. The low-back chairs provide comfortable seating without blocking the windows on three sides.

At the living room end in the foreground was just enough room for a sofa, lounge chair (not visible in photo), and antique spool chest to cluster around the fireplace.

Finally, the homeowners decided to sacrifice some light and a not-so-great view by showcasing their prized antique rolltop desk in front of a living room window. If your room seems to have a surfeit of windows, you might want to consider ignoring one.

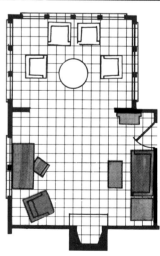

SOLVING PLAN PROBLEMS: TOO MANY FOCAL POINTS

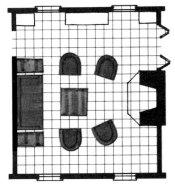

Seeing double isn't funny when you're looking at two focal points in a room. One focal point is essential, two create confusion. The living room *above* had both a fireplace and an impressive window/storage wall. Either could serve as the room's focal point. But if you study the plan *at left,* you'll see why this room features the focal point it does.

Dramatic as the window wall is, doorways on both sides make the area in front of the windows a natural corridor for traffic—hardly what you'd want moving through your conversation area. This made the fireplace the logical focal point to develop a furniture grouping around. But there's more to the story here than that. Shrewd furniture arranging makes the best possible use of both feature areas.

The right furniture in the right places lets the window wall continue to play a strong supporting role in the room's design. With the sofa placed against the wall opposite the fireplace, and chairs in between, nearly every seat is the best in the house; almost everyone can enjoy the warmth of the fireplace or the light and design elements of the storage system. The room also has a good balance of visual weight—the sofa, fireplace, and window wall all anchor the scheme. To keep things from becoming too heavy and massive, light-scaled, open chairs flank the sofa. The low, sculptured shapes don't block the view of either focal point.

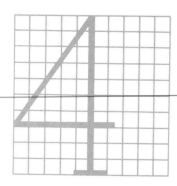

DOUBLING UP
LETS A ROOM
DO MORE

It's a rare room that serves a single purpose anymore. Smaller houses, condominiums, and apartments challenge us to wring maximum usefulness out of every inch of space. One of the best ways to do this is to double (or triple, or quadruple) the activities a room can handle. This chapter moves through your home—from "public" spaces such as dining and family rooms to personal domains shared by just one or two persons—telling how you can persuade part- or even full-time areas to take on another job or two.

A room best serves more than one purpose when disparate functions are somehow separated. Strategically placed, a sofa, some shelving, a desk, even a bed can act as a peninsula that divides a room's activities.

In the case of the room shown *at right,* a king-size bed, custom headboard-and-shelving unit, and pair of niches divide the space into three sections. One niche includes a hideaway desk, the other a handy grooming center. And just to take a good idea one step further to better, the bed itself doubles for lounging while you watch TV or enjoy a cup of tea.

Sofas are good dividers, too. Place one perpendicular to a wall and you can create a sitting area on one side, a home office, music corner, or other amenity on the other. A desk, similarly placed, can establish a work oasis in an otherwise busy living room or family room.

Other peninsula options

If you need a bit more division than a piece of furniture can provide, try shelving. Shelves with either see-through or solid backs can put a wall where none existed before, partitioning off a dining area, a crafts center, or a reading nook—to name just three possibilities.

Just about any room in your house can gain from division. In a combination kitchen-dining area, for example, a peninsula-style counter puts a psychological barrier between eating and work areas, yet the two remain totally accessible to each other.

DOUBLING UP LETS A ROOM DO MORE

DINING ROOMS

If your dining room sits idle between meals, you may be missing out on a lot of space-stretching potential. Whether you have the luxury of a separate dining room, or are forced to dine in a room that already has other duties, careful thought—and maybe a few new pieces of furniture—can give that room a double or even triple identity.

Your dining room's possibilities for another life are limited only by your imagination and your family's needs. Want a home office, game room, sewing center, library, guest room? Any of these functions and more can be added to a dining area, even if it's nothing more than a modest "L" off your living room. First let's look at what you can do with a separate room, then consider how you can incorporate eating space into an area that's already doing something else.

Turning tables
The most prominent item in any dining room is a table —and a table is too important a work surface to be ignored. Good planning can put it to use all day long.

If you need a desk, sewing, or crafts center, simply provide nearby storage capability that can free the table for dining, and vice versa. If there's room, a hutch or armoire may be the answer; if not, put the walls themselves to work.

Walls lined with shelving can serve a host of duties. Open shelves accommodate books and collectibles; some, kept clear, can double for serving. Add doors, and you create china cabinets or stashing space for hobby stuff you want to keep out of the way.

If your dining table expands, keep it at its smallest; you'll free maximum floor space, and the table will be just the right size for desk, hobby, or game use.

Don't think a table has to sit exactly in the middle of a room, either. Push it to one side and the floor space you gain could accommodate a small sitting area, furnished, say, with a pair of wing chairs, or a small loveseat that might also hide a foldout guest bed.

Or, instead of one table, consider two smaller ones. These could serve many functions, then butt together as one large surface for mealtime gatherings.

Once an underemployed dining room, the family room/library shown *at left* now employs several of the strategies we've just discussed. Moving the table against a wall has liberated the rest of the space for comfortable seating. Built-in shelving lines virtually every inch of wall space. The table serves as a buffet, or expands for serving occasional large, sit-down dinners.

Dining in disguise
Where no separate dining area exists, take the opposite approach to eke out dining space. For this situation, dual-purpose furniture comes into play: a flip-top or drop-leaf sofa table assumes dining duty; the base of a high-low table rotates to adjust from cocktail to dining height; a game table with extensible ends expands for dining; a sizable table folds up Murphy-bed style into a modular storage system or console buffet. (More about these quick-change artists on pages 69-71.)

Whatever your table disguise, its chairs can double as occasional seating or transfer to other locations throughout the house. Fold-up and stacking chairs offer two other means for removing seating when it's unneeded.

FAMILY ROOMS

Well-planned family rooms go way beyond double duty. The very best are let-your-hair-down, put-your-feet-up places that serve multitudinous activities. And just as there is no such thing as the "typical" American family with its two-and-a-fraction children, neither is there a typical family room. Each and every family room should spring from the interests of the family that lives there.

How many needs your family room serves, and how well, depends on the groundwork you lay. If your family doesn't now have a special space, your first priority is to establish one. It may be adjacent to the kitchen, in a refurbished basement, an attic, a converted garage, or an enclosed porch. (For more about all of these possibilities, see chapters 5, 6, and 7.)

Next, inventory the activities likely to take place in your family room. If you have small children, you'll want to include a place for play, with ample storage to hide toys when the adults take over.

The reclaimed basement shown on these pages, for example, magically converts from a quiet adult retreat to a children's fantasy land. Deft sleight of hand makes custom built-ins in the storage wall and under the stairs into much more than they seem, thanks to plywood doors that have been painted with a playhouse motif on their inside surfaces.

Older kids and teens need a spot where they can entertain friends; ideally it should include TV, music equipment, and a floor that is suitable for dancing.

If your family has an artist or hobbyist, you may want work space, and perhaps gallery or display space, as well. You could even incorporate in your plan an entire workshop concealable behind closed doors when not in use.

Few pieces, many uses
No family room should lack a table for games, informal meals, homework, or hobby projects. Equally important is comfortable, curl-up seating. This might be built in, with storage underneath. Or consider arranging a couple of twin beds L-fashion in a corner.

They cost less than a sectional sofa of comparable size. Backed with bolsters and throw pillows, they're almost as comfortable, and of course you have quarters for overnight guests.

If you're going to go ahead with a sofa or sectional instead, by all means invest in a sofa bed. For still more sleeping space, look at other pieces —such as chairs and ottomans —that convert into beds as well. (For further details on these convertibles, see pages 70 and 71.)

Surfaces and storage
As you plan your family room, make sure everything—from flooring to fabrics to wall covering—is as durable and maintenance-free as possible. Very few active people today will feel comfortable in an environment as delicate as Aunt Lydia's parlor.

Finally, think of all the things you'll want to keep in your family room—books, games, hobby supplies, TV set, stereo equipment, records (the list could go on and on). Carefully estimate the amount of storage you need, then double it; you will find that whatever space you have left over will fill very quickly.

As with seating, storage can be built-in or freestanding. Just make sure it's flexible. Children's pursuits change as the children grow older; so, often, do adults'.

BEDROOMS

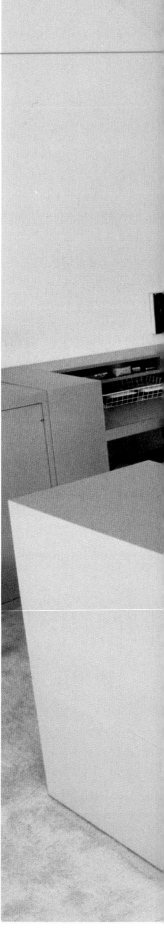

Long for a quiet place to curl up with a good book, enjoy music, or watch TV? How about a private desk for correspondence and household record-keeping, a spot to sew, or an intimate conversation area? Any or all these activities can happen in a bedroom designed for around-the-clock functioning.

Bedrooms begin with a bed, but they need not end there. With just a tailored or fitted spread strewn with pillows, you can turn your bed into a pillowed sofa by day. Or, in place of a spread, "upholster" both the mattress and box springs in fitted sheets, then place all directly on the floor. Store bedding in wicker or wood trunks that also serve as end tables.

Realize, too, that beds need not go in a corner or up against a wall. Try "floating" a double or queen-size bed—perhaps diagonally—in the middle of the floor. With large bolster pillows lined up down the center you have back-to-back seating.

To add greater comfort to your bedroom than it has now, develop a space for a small conversation grouping—two chairs, a small table, and maybe a loveseat. If your room also has a fine view, place a pair of lounge chairs face to face along a window, with a shared ottoman between to serve as a double *chaise longue*. And don't forget to provide good reading lamps.

Even the tiniest bedroom can likely accommodate a table or desk for work space, especially if it doubles as a night stand; a drop-leaf table works well in this situation.

Engineering your sleep space

Probably the ultimate way to wake up a bedroom is with a sleek modular system like the one pictured *at right.* In a modest-size bedroom it incorporates desk space for two along with plenty of storage for clothes, office supplies, and even extra bedding (in the flip-top headboard). A 39-inch-high footboard divides the sleeping space from a small sitting area beyond, and houses a TV, video recorder, and stereo system, as shown in the photo *below.*

DOUBLING UP LETS A ROOM DO MORE

To children, the last thing a bedroom is, is a place to sleep. Rather, it's a personal world, a place to play, fantasize, pursue hobbies, stow secrets, escape, socialize. And unless you plan to redecorate every third year or so, furnishings should be flexible and tough enough to "grow up," too.

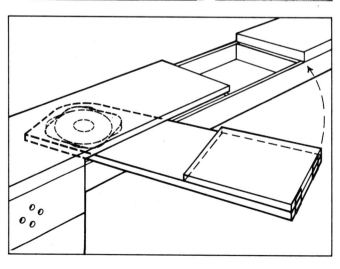

Even a room planned just for sleeping will lead a multipurpose life if a child is in residence. Youngsters instinctively find uses for furniture that adults might never dream of. A toddler sees a chair as something to climb on or hide behind. The floor is a natural work surface in the eyes of a kindergartner. The vivid imagination of a school-age child can turn an open bookshelf into a puppet stage. Observe kids in action and you'll quickly see what furnishings will best suit their needs.

The prerequisites of furnishings for a child's room are fairly simple: look for safety first, then durable and sturdy construction, and flexibility for future use.

Besides a bed, kids need floor space for play, a table or desk-top work surface, good light, clothes storage, and plenty of stashing space. (The better planned this last is, the more easily you can encourage your children to keep their rooms neat and organized.)

Divide for harmonious double occupancy

When two or more children share a room, your challenge intensifies. Space for playing together is not enough. Each child also needs privacy—best accomplished with room dividers such as screens, free-standing storage units, or ceiling-hung bamboo shades. At the very least, each child should have a separate, clearly defined place for playing, studying, and sleeping.

Bunks and trundles conserve floor space in rooms that billet two or more. Some come with shelves, chests, or desk cubbyholes beneath; the kind that can separate for future use as twin beds or couches —cornered and dressed with bolsters and tailored spreads —will be the most versatile.

Unfinished furniture + imagination = low-budget function

A clever combination of store-bought and hand-built items can turn a tiny corner into a full room, as illustrated in the photos and drawing *opposite*. The ready-made platform bed, specially made plywood shelves and three-drawer chests combine as a fully functioning, private place for study, storage, and just plain lounging. Here, the star attraction is a swing-out table that folds up and pivots to stow away in the shelf, as shown in the drawing; to ease handling, the complete assembly pivots on a ball-bearing turntable.

For a novel way to expand a child's room, consider annexing the closet. That's what the parents of a teenage daughter did to create the makeup center pictured *at right*. They simply removed the doors and reorganized storage with store-bought wire shelving units. Her vanity table consists of two tiers of plastic cylindrical storage units that are topped with particleboard.

One big advantage to modular units such as the ones shown here is that they can be organized to provide low table and desk surfaces for small children, then later rearranged to make higher ones as the children grow.

MULTIPURPOSE FURNITURE

We've said it again and again throughout this book: when you need to stretch living space, think multipurpose. Multipurpose furniture not only conserves precious space, it also broadens your options for the future. These pages introduce you to the versatility of multipurpose furniture; pages 70 and 71 tell what you need to know when you're shopping for multipurpose pieces.

First, let's straighten out some terminology. Multipurpose furniture falls into two broad categories. *Convertible* pieces—such as sofa beds—serve two or sometimes three different functions. *Modular* furniture comes in cubes or other shapes that you can array, like building blocks, in just about any way you like.

In other words, convertibles are versatile, modulars even more so. This doesn't mean, however, that you should automatically favor modulars over convertibles. The sleep sofa, for instance, is a classic destined to endure.

What's more, sleepers such as the one pictured *opposite* can also play a part in a modular grouping. These twins can butt together end to end, sit opposite each other, or fit into a corner, as shown. Once the 52x70-inch mattress is folded away, you are unable to tell which unit has the bed.

Not all sleepers are sofas anymore, either; you can also find them in benches, chests, and chairs, and in wall-storage units that flip down like Mr. Murphy's original invention. Modular furniture comes in even more diverse shapes than do convertibles. The most basic modulars are floor pillows: they provide extra seating when you need it, stack out of the way when you don't. Lay three pillows out flat, and you also have a child-size bed.

Modulars for grown-ups include chair- or sofa-size units that can be arranged and rearranged into a number of

seating configurations, collected about a table, incorporated into built-in settings, or teamed with conventional chairs.

Tables, too

Convertible tables also can do double duty. The high/low version shown *above* and *at right* serves as a sturdy, 16-inch-high coffee table; adjust its chrome legs and it rises to an adult dining or desk height.

Dining tables also come disguised as end tables, hall consoles, desks, buffets, even walls—thanks to flip-up, fold-out mechanisms.

Storing and more

Multipurpose means magic for storage as well as seating and tables. Modular units are especially attractive because you can assemble them in stages. Rather than buy an entire wall system at once (and possibly go broke doing it), you might start out with a single bookcase or bar unit and add others later as you can afford them. Best of all, modulars are always ready to move on—whether it's to another room or a new home. *(continued)*

SELECTING MULTIPURPOSE FURNITURE

(continued)

Any furniture purchase represents an investment you expect to live with for years to come. And since multipurpose pieces may be doing different jobs tomorrow from the ones you anticipate today, durability becomes very important —you want items that will last long enough to let you cash in on their future flexibility. Here is how to buy with an eye to quality as well as to versatility.

When you're shopping for multipurpose furniture, try to analyze how a piece will perform in each of the ways you'll likely use it. Most furniture does some jobs better than other jobs. But beware of pieces that promise to serve 15 different functions—they often end up doing none of them very well.

Also, as with any major consumer item, go for the best quality you can afford, and stick to reliable brands and reputable dealers. If budget is a problem, consider allocating most of it for a few good items, and temporarily fill in with inexpensive expendables such as colorful cardboard boxes or thrift-store bargains.

Sleeper savvy
Today's convertible sofas hide their second lives so well that to make sure about many, you'll probably have to ask. You can't tell a sleeper just by looking at it or sitting on it anymore. And as we've already mentioned, sleepers are no longer limited to sofas. Nowadays you can pull a bed out of just about anything short of a top hat.

In a sleeper the mattress—be it foam or innerspring—unfolds at the tug of a handle. Sleeper mattresses come in widths ranging from twin- to queen-size, but if length is critical, shop carefully; foldaway mattresses often measure only 72 inches long, rather than the

80- to 84-inch lengths typical of conventional mattresses.

Because a sofa bed is considerably heavier than a regular sofa, look for one equipped with good casters so you can move it easily. For even more mobility, consider a sofa or chair bed constructed largely

of foam; these simply unfold into bed-size slabs that lie directly on the floor.

Who would guess, for example, that the good-looking chair shown *opposite bottom* flips out to make the 30x75-inch bed pictured *opposite top.*

Whatever you opt for, be sure you get the comfort you need. If a piece will be used mainly for seating, sitting comfort is paramount; if it is for nightly sleeping, a premium innerspring mattress may be well worth the extra cost, even if it makes the sofa a bit firmer than you'd prefer.

Making modulars work
Once strictly contemporary-looking blocks, modular seating now comes in traditional and transitional styles as well. The trickiest part of selecting modulars is determining the number of units—corners, armless, ottomans, and so forth—that your room can accommodate. The best way to do this is to draw the room to scale and experiment with paper cutouts of the modules you have in mind, as explained in Chapter 3. (Templates at the back of this book—pages 152-157—give standard dimensions for modular furniture.)

Casing case pieces
Case pieces—unupholstered furniture such as cabinets and chests, desks, armoires, wall

units, headboards, and tables —may be constructed of solid wood or veneer, plastic or metal, wicker or rattan, or a combination of these.

With multi-function in mind, choose cabinets and chests that can live separately, bunch together, or stack to conserve floor space.

Modular wall systems can climb the wall for maximum capacity, or line up at desk level around the room; with many you can incorporate a desk, bar, headboard, display space, even lighting.

The handsome unit shown *top left* and *above* is a case in

point. When it's time to get down to business, the flip-up top opens to reveal a drop-down desk.

Insist on durability
Make sure that any furniture you select is sturdy enough to take the use you'll be giving it. Case pieces should have absolutely no wobble or flex. Modular units should fit together snugly. Chair and sofa backs shouldn't give when you lean back. The bed in a sleeper should not rock when you sit on it.

The fabric you settle on depends in part upon what you're willing to pay—fabric prices vary widely—and on the punishment you expect a

piece to receive. Some colors hide dirt and wear better than others; stain-repellent finishes make sense in heavy-use rooms. Check to ensure that seams are tightly stitched, patterns carefully matched.

For hard surfaces, plastic laminate is the most resistant and easy to clean. If you prefer wood, choose distressed or oiled finishes for easiest care; paint and lacquer clean easily, but mar even more easily. Kids' furniture should be smooth and able to take rough treatment, and come with safely rounded corners and a high resistance to tipping.

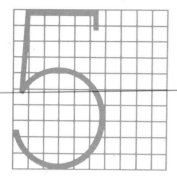

STRUCTURAL SURGERY

If your house suffers from boxy, closed-in spaces, maybe an operation is in order. You'll need a wrecking bar instead of a scalpel, but removing a wall or two, cutting in a new window, or raising a ceiling to the rafters may be just what the doctor ordered. This chapter tells about each of these surgical techniques, and visits several homes that lead happier, more open lives after their architectural operations.

Knocking out a wall or two can be an inexpensive way to gain more elbowroom, and give the inside of your house a whole new look almost overnight. But before you get out the wrecking bar, realize that removing walls calls for careful planning, and can create a good deal of mess and inconvenience. What's more, you could quite literally bring down the house. This is why you should always seek advice from an architect or contractor before you begin whacking away.

You also may need to work out some special advance arrangements. For example, you may need to hire and schedule the services of an electrician, a finish carpenter, or a plumbing and heating contractor. And you may have to dispose of debris yourself—many garbage collection services don't accept building rubble.

Assess your walls

Whether or not you do the work yourself, determine beforehand what any wall in question does for your house's structure. Basically, walls are of two types: those that only enclose space, and those that also support what's overhead.

The anatomy drawing, *opposite,* shows cutaway views of both. *Non-bearing* walls typically run parallel with the joist framing above them; *bearing* (or supporting) walls usually run perpendicular to the joists. Also, bearing walls stand directly over other bearing walls —or beams—that are beneath the floor, so the weight is supported all the way down to the foundation.

Both types of walls are generally constructed of 2x4 *studs* spaced 16 or 24 inches apart, with a 2x4 *top plate* above (bearing walls often have two), and a *bottom* or *toe plate* of

2x4s below. The interior surfaces are covered with either *drywall*—plaster sandwiched between two layers of heavy paper—or *lath* and *plaster.*

Taking out a non-bearing wall is a dusty but not especially difficult job. First shut off any wiring or plumbing that runs through the wall, then pry away trim such as baseboards or door frames. Now put on goggles, a helmet, and heavy gloves, and begin smacking the wall surface with a sledgehammer or wrecking bar. You can easily break right through drywall, then pull material off the studs; with plaster and lath, break the plaster loose first, then pry away the lath. Prepare for a lot of dust and heavy debris when the plaster comes down.

Next, pull nails holding the studs at top or bottom, and yank the studs free. Finally, pry off the plates and haul out the debris you've created.

Removing a bearing wall

When you remove a bearing wall, you have to substitute something to carry the weight. This is a job for a professional, who may recommend one of the two options shown, *bottom, opposite.*

If the span is no more than 12 feet and you want continuous wall and ceiling surfaces, install a *laminated* beam mounted flush within the ceiling framework.

If continuous planes aren't important, or if the span will exceed 12 feet, you might opt for a *truss* consisting of two planks with spacers between them. The ends of the truss rest on stub walls at each side of the new opening.

If the span will be more than 15 feet, support either support system with posts spaced at intervals along the span.

(continued)

ANATOMY OF A NON-BEARING WALL (left) AND A BEARING WALL (right)

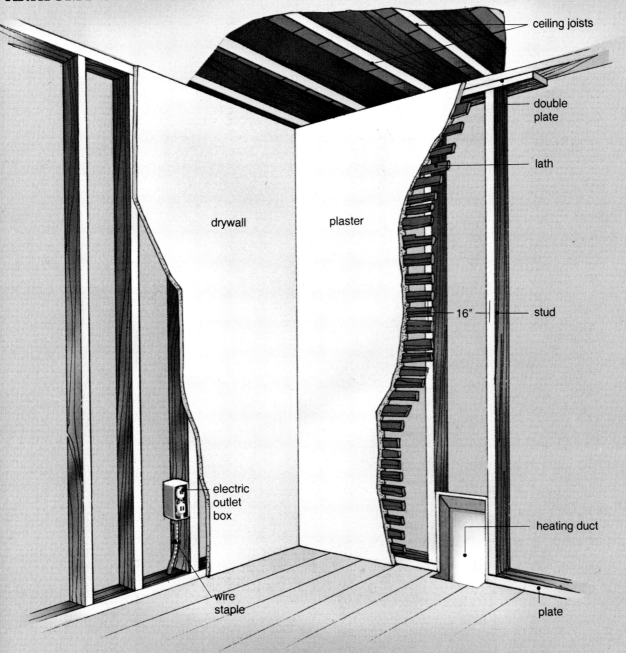

ceiling joists

double plate

lath

drywall

plaster

16"

stud

electric outlet box

heating duct

wire staple

plate

BEARING WALL SUBSTITUTES: LAMINATED BEAM (left); TRUSS (right)

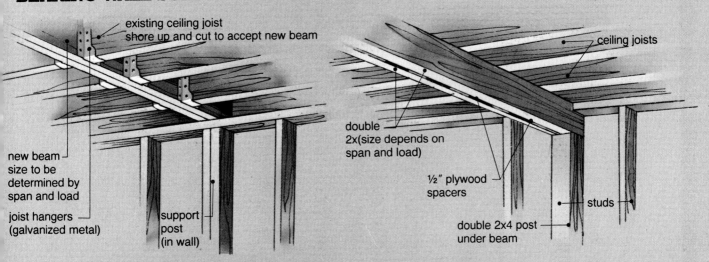

existing ceiling joist shore up and cut to accept new beam

ceiling joists

double 2x(size depends on span and load)

½" plywood spacers

new beam size to be determined by span and load

studs

joist hangers (galvanized metal)

support post (in wall)

double 2x4 post under beam

DOWN WITH WALLS

(continued)

Almost nothing surpasses the thrill of breaking through a wall and seeing formerly separate spaces merge into a new world of possibilities. You add only the few square inches occupied by the old wall—yet suddenly your home seems bigger, brighter, airier, with more room to move and live. You can shift furniture to suit your needs, rather than the other way around; and your whole family can congregate comfortably for a daily sharing of experiences. The home pictured here shows just how appealing an open room can be.

Examine the "before" plan, *below,* and you can see how too many walls created a series of chunky rooms at the back of the house, each visually isolated from the others. Removing a couple of walls and a closet changed all that into the free-flowing living/dining area pictured, *opposite.*

In the photo *opposite top* you'll see where beams now take up the load formerly carried by walls. One beam, extending to the left just above the clock, is recessed into the ceiling; the second beam is incorporated in a dropped ceiling over the new sliding glass doors.

Bigger rooms mean more versatility

Now the larger space easily accommodates family activities or a big party. At one end, *opposite top,* is dining space for six or eight; at the other, *opposite bottom,* a fireplace and roomy conversation area. Thanks to the absence of visual barriers, neither area seems confining or over-furnished. Plenty of space remains for traffic to circulate freely, plus enough wall space for storage and a varied collection of prints and accent pieces.

Big spaces have another compelling feature: you can decorate them boldly. Bright colors, striking architectural treatments, and large-scale furnishings or art works don't appear overwhelming or out of proportion in expansive rooms.

Opening up the whole house

Be sure to note how a new room relates to the rest of the house. In this house, wide archways and continuity of finish materials make the new area a natural extension of others, and the sliding glass doors seem to extend the interior space into the garden. (For more information about windows and sliding glass doors refer to pages 78-83.)

Removing just one wall can affect relationships among your home's interior spaces, which underscores the importance of careful planning. How will traffic patterns change? How will removing a wall affect the room's natural lighting and the movement of air? Could another alteration or two make the scheme work even better? If you have any doubts about your ability to envision these or other consequences, consult an architect before that wall comes down.   *(continued)*

AFTER THE DUST SETTLES

If the wall to be removed was added after your house was constructed, consider yourself lucky. Probably its top and bottom plates simply were nailed to the existing floor and ceiling, and you'll be left with just a few small holes to fill.

If, on the other hand, the wall was built *before* surface materials were installed—as most are—prepare to spend more time patching gaps in the ceiling, floor, and adjacent walls than you did demolishing the partition.

Unless you're handy with a trowel, leave plaster work to a pro. With patience, you can piece in drywall yourself. Cut back to studs on either side of the gap, cut sections to fit, and cover the seams with joint tape and compound.

With flooring you have a couple of choices. One is to fill in the gap with any piece of wood that's the right width and thickness, then recover the entire merged area with carpeting, resilient goods, or other new flooring material.

Or, if you can find a few pieces of new wood flooring that match the old, piece them in, sand, and refinish the entire surface. Boards that run perpendicular to the now-removed wall will have to be cut back and stagger-jointed.

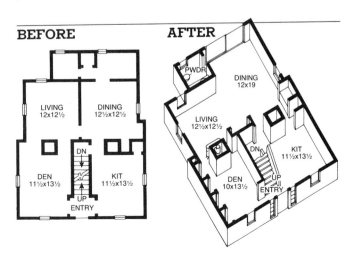

BEFORE

LIVING 12x12½
DINING 12½x12½
DEN 11½x13½
KIT 11½x13½
DN
UP
ENTRY

AFTER

PWDR
DINING 12x19
LIVING 12½x12½
DN
KIT 11½x13½
DEN 10x13½
UP
ENTRY

DOWN WITH WALLS

(continued)

The key to understanding what happened here is to focus on the core of the "before" plan. Originally a staircase climbed up around the fireplace, separating the kitchen from the living room and a squarish formal dining room. Main rooms sat like orphans, isolated by the stairs and fireplace, and a hodge-podge of walls and jogs.

To meld everything into one large space, the stairs have been relocated, and the interior walls replaced by beams and a system of posts. Four of the posts replace walls that had surrounded the fireplace, and now support previously existing beams in the living room ceiling, *far right*.

Within its new "four-poster" frame, the white-painted chimney provides a sculptural centerpiece that divides the new space into zones, each borrowing visually from the others. On all sides, each area is finished in the same simple fashion: wood flooring, simple furnishings, and off-white walls.

Now the kitchen is at the heart of the house

Just behind the fireplace, and slightly to one side, is the new core—the kitchen, *near right*. It fits neatly into a triangular space that affords unobstructed views of the dining area and part of the living area. At the apex of the kitchen's work-area triangle, the cook can stay in touch with family and guests, yet remain within arm's reach of the sink, stove, dishwasher, and cupboards.

Here, replacing the old walls, is a truss-style beam that spans the diagonal side of the work center. Beneath the beam, a diagonal counter defines the work area and conceals kitchen clutter without obstructing the view.

The structural surgery that brought about this transformation amounted to a major operation. Moving stairways, installing support posts and beams, and making other major alterations are all jobs well beyond the capability of a weekend do-it-yourselfer. Besides, who'd want to live here while the work proceeded? If your budget is tight, consider hiring a contractor to do the demolition and support work, then finish off the new spaces on your own.

BEFORE

AFTER

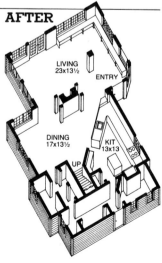

Imagine what your home might be like without any interior walls. Now fill in the blank spaces only where you really need division—to partition off bedrooms and baths, for instance. That's what happened in this turn-of-the-century house when four rooms became one wide-open space. Now only a few beams, four handsome posts, and a once-buried brick fireplace and chimney interrupt the home's interior space.

BRING IN
MORE LIGHT

Another effective antidote for a house that seems closed in is to borrow "extra" light and space from the outdoors. But, you ask, don't new windows and, especially, sliding glass doors increase heat losses and add to a home's energy load? The answer depends on how you orient glass areas and whether you cover them when the sun isn't shining. Properly insulated, south- and east-facing windows often gain more heat than they lose, making them passive solar collectors. More about this on page 81. Let's look at a window's major components and how a window fits into a wall.

Installing a new window or sliding glass door is a moderately difficult to difficult job, depending mainly on what covers the exterior of your home. Window units come prehung in frames that simply plug into "rough" openings. All your carpenter or you have to do is make the opening and brace the wall properly. The photograph and anatomy drawings here show what is involved.

Start from the inside, removing drywall or plaster and lath all the way from the floor to the ceiling; even if you're putting in a small window, you'll need to get at the wall framing both above and below.

Now move outside and make your exterior cut to the dimensions specified by the window or door manufacturer. Probably the framing is sheathed with boards or asbestos panels under a veneer of masonry or siding. There also may be a layer of heavy building paper over board-type sheathing or under masonry. If the opening will be wider than 3 feet, brace the ceiling inside before cutting away studs.

The standard framing technique for openings consists of a *header* nailed between two full-length studs and supported by extra *trimmers* on either side. For openings up to 3½ feet wide, make your header from a pair of 2x4s with ½-inch spacers nailed between; wider openings call for a 2x6 header. If your house has a masonry veneer, you'll also need a steel *lintel* above.

For windows, the bottom of the opening is framed with a double 2x4 nailed into the trimmers and supported by short studs underneath. For doors, the *toe plate* is cut away and the existing subfloor serves as the bottom of the opening.

(continued)

ANATOMY OF A SLIDING
GLASS DOOR

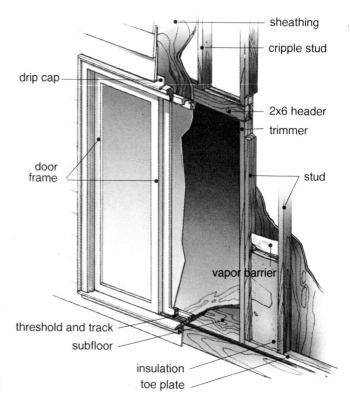

sheathing

cripple stud

drip cap

2x6 header

trimmer

door
frame

stud

vapor barrier

threshold and track

subfloor

insulation

toe plate

ANATOMY OF A CASEMENT WINDOW

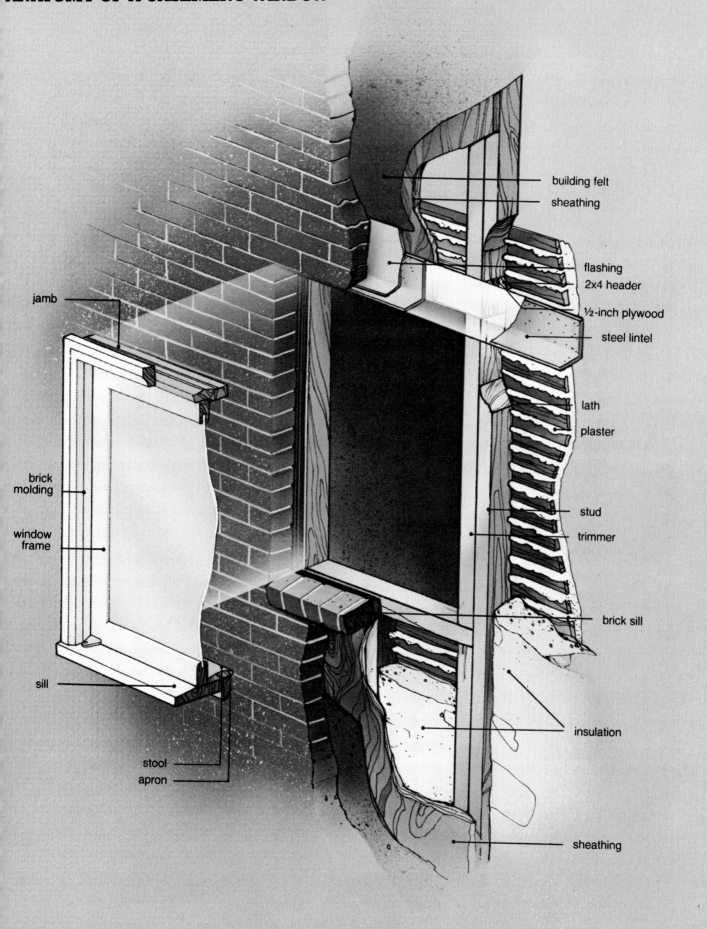

building felt

sheathing

flashing

2x4 header

½-inch plywood

steel lintel

lath

plaster

stud

trimmer

brick sill

insulation

sheathing

jamb

brick molding

window frame

sill

stool

apron

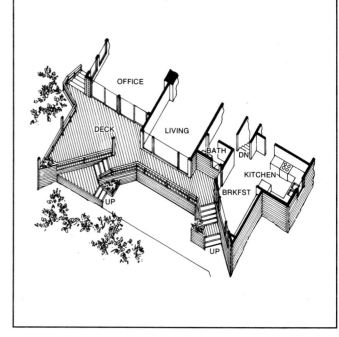

BRING IN MORE LIGHT

(continued)

Open up a room that's small and dark, and you gain a whole new outlook on life. With just a small investment of time, money, and effort you get a view, a room bathed with light, or, maybe even better, access to outdoor living areas. Of course, the type of window you install depends a great deal on what you want it to do. Here is how to pick the best way to go.

Like people, windows come in many shapes and sizes, and some do some tasks better than other tasks. To choose the right window for the job you have in mind, ask yourself a few basic questions. Do you primarily need more light, or is the view equally important? What about privacy and ventilation? Most important, what will the new window do for your home's heating and cooling bills?

If light is of paramount consideration, consider stretching the opening all the way to the ceiling. It needn't drop to floor level, however; light entering near the floor only illuminates a few square feet down there. For even more light, bump out the opening a foot or two and create a glass-roofed bay like the one shown *opposite top*.

In rooms where a view isn't important, a skylight or high window may be all you need. A horizontal window high on a wall may actually provide more light than the same window turned vertically—and give much more privacy.

Even when you want to capitalize on a view, determine the size and placement of openings carefully. To conserve energy and your privacy, for instance, a small window that frames only the best part of a view or focuses on landscaping in the foreground may make better sense than a larger window would.

If ventilation isn't critical, fixed panes can save money. Or consider opting for moveable sections only at the top, bottom, or sides. Be sure to choose a unit that lets in the right amount of air and opens to snag passing breezes.

A need for more light, view, and access to the outdoors led to the dramatic opening-up pictured *opposite*. Main living areas were once walled in be-

ORIENTING WINDOWS FOR ENERGY EFFICIENCY

Yes, your home can have a view and stay warm, too—if you synchronize your needs for light and views with nature's highly predictable patterns.

In this hemisphere the sun's warmest rays come from the south, and cold comes mainly from the north. Since the sun is both your ally and enemy, capture it in winter and block it in summer. This means openings for light and warmth should face primarily south, secondarily west and east, and lastly north.

When you add a window, think of it as a dynamic item rather than a fixed one. Screens, draperies, roof overhangs, and other barriers let you control a window's role in absorbing or dissipating heat. Deciduous trees can do the same, automatically. Leaves shade windows in summer, drop to let sunlight through in the fall and winter.

Where does the wind come from?

Consider the direction of prevailing winds as well. Cold air blowing against unprotected windows magnifies energy losses. During the summer the reverse is true: cooling breezes provide ventilation that will

help reduce your need for air conditioning.

Don't overlook ventilation, either. Ideally, the best cross-ventilation happens when inlets and outlets for air are on opposite sides of the house and the passage between them is as unobstructed as possible. Size the outlet larger than the inlet and you will increase the velocity of the air moving through. Lower openings provide better cooling than higher ones—but be sure you also have adequate outlets upstairs under the roof, where the greatest heat buildups occur.

What kind of windows?

Don't settle for anything less than double-glazing, and triple-glazing is even better. A second layer of glass reduces heat transmission by as much as 50 percent; a storm window or a third layer of glass ups that to 67 percent.

Finally, keep energy in mind at the time you install a new window, and afterward. Fit the new unit snugly into its rough opening; insulate and caulk the air spaces on all sides. To reduce nighttime heat losses, cover the window with close-fitting draperies or extra-thick shades.

hind conventionally sized windows. The wooded site made rooms seem especially dark in summer, and the lawn, trees, and shrubs could only be glimpsed piecemeal through one window at a time.

The owners had already decided to add an eating area, so they popped out the kitchen with a triangular mini-addition, then broke open walls in the living room and home office.
(continued)

BRING IN
MORE LIGHT
(continued)

Thinking about converting your attic, porch, or garage into more living space? Don't forget to bring in extra light there, too. An unfinished space offers a rare opportunity to try bold, imaginative solutions, because you can start completely from scratch. And since the walls and the roof in these spaces usually are exterior surfaces, you're free to scoop in light wherever and however you please. Each of the light-grabbers on these pages turned an old dust-catcher into sun-splashed living space.

The inviting greenhouse-style alcove, *opposite,* was once an unheated porch. The owners brought it in from the cold by taking out the interior wall and raising the floor level to that of the interior. Then they turned the entire space into a giant light scoop and direct-gain heat trap by pushing the ceiling to the roof line and adding several domed skylights. To preserve a sense of openness and easy access, they also installed floor-to-ceiling fixed glass panels and a pair of glass doors in the long exterior wall, and painted the walls and ceilings white. (For more information about converting porches, go to pages 112-117.)

Solar heat for a former garage

A garage remodeling may call for a different bag of tricks. Since a garage already has at least one large opening—for the door—usually wall-sized, your main challenge becomes how to fill it.

One ingenious family made the old door openings do double duty, *upper right.* When they converted their two-car garage into extra bedroom space, they bumped out the openings and transformed them into studio-style bay windows.

The bays serve not only as light scoops, but also as passive solar collectors; the glazing slants outward at the bottom to trap the sun's heat and warm the annexed space. Heavy shades pull up from the bottom in each bay to provide privacy and to reduce heat loss at night. (More about garage conversions on pages 104-111.)

Brightening an attic

Skylights are a natural for lighting and warming up attics.

Space that's now tucked in out of sight under the roof can become just as bright and sunny as the rest of the house—often even more so.

In the attic remodeling pictured here, *lower right,* the south slope of the roof was opened up with several extra-long skylights that fit between the rafters. Insulated with double glazing, the skylights help trap the sun's warmth. Insulated skylights come in various sizes and shapes, so you are likely to find at least one that's just right for your roof and attic space. Some types are operable and equipped with self-storing screens for ventilation. Insulated units also are available with tinted glass or built-in, roll-up shades to reduce heat gain in summer. (For more about attics and skylights turn to pages 96-103.)

REACH UP

Some room stretchers work by fooling the eye; others actually add space—space already available if you know where to look for it. One of the best places to look is up—to your attic. There you may have hundreds of cubic feet going to waste. Even if the roof pitch is fairly shallow, you can make that bonus space work so your closed-in rooms look bigger. And, if there's at least a little headroom, you can create a whole new living level while you're at it.

Removing a ceiling requires consultation with an architect or engineer, but you can probably do most of the actual work yourself. And you can get a jump on the professionals by checking out your attic in advance. If it has no subfloor, haul up a few boards to crawl around on—unless you enjoy coming down the hard way. Check for any heating, plumbing, or electrical components that might have to be relocated. If your house has no basement, heating ducts may run over or between the ceiling joists you plan to remove; electrical cables may be strung between the joists, hidden under a layer of insulation. (Before you check the wiring, turn off power to that part of the house.)

While you're up there, note the location of vents in the gables or along the roof peak. You may have to seal up and replace them with new vents elsewhere. What type of insulation, if any, is there now between the joists? If it's in batts or rolls, you probably can reuse it.

Finally, determine the kind of framework used in your attic. In residential construction, roof framing is one of two basic types, shown in the drawings, *opposite.*

Traditional construction: rafters and joists
The older and more common roof framing, *top drawing,* is made up of 2x6 or 2x8 *rafters* notched into the walls at the bottom and joined by a *ridge beam* at the top. The floor of the attic (and the ceiling of the rooms below) is framed with 2x4, 2x6, or 2x8 *joists* that rest on top of the wall and that join the bottom ends of the rafters. Both the joists and rafters are

spaced 16 inches apart from center to center. The rafters are also reinforced near the top with *ties* or *collars* to keep them from collapsing under their own weight and the added weight of the roof.

In older houses, the rafters usually are *sheathed* with boards, and the ceiling under the joists is constructed of *lath* and *plaster.* In houses built since the mid-1940s, the sheathing is plywood and the ceiling is drywall. Directly above the drywall is a layer of plastic sheeting that forms part of the vapor barrier.

Construction today: truss systems
If your house was built within the last 20 years, its attic may have been framed with trusses, *bottom illustration,* instead of rafters and joists. Trusses are constructed from 2x4s spliced together with metal *connectors* and with nails. The girder-like design of trusses makes them strong enough to span the full width of the house. They can be spaced 24 inches on center rather than 16, and they require no ridge-beam connection at the peak. Combined with plywood sheathing they form a very stable structural system.

In residential construction, truss systems are most commonly used for houses with low-pitched roofs—the attic they enclose isn't intended for living space. Therefore, no joists are necessary; drywall ceilings are nailed to the bottoms of the trusses and a plastic *vapor barrier* and insulation are laid between the trusses, on top of the drywall.

Reaching up with a cathedral ceiling
How you plan to reach up depends on what you find. Let's take the simple example of annexing part of the attic for a cathedral ceiling.

If the attic framing consists of rafters and joists, you'll need to determine how much the framing system depends on cross ties and joists for stability in that part of the house (at this point you'll need to call in an architect or engineer). Usually joists do nothing more than hold up the ceiling, but if you want to remove any of the cross ties you'll probably have to substitute something else— such as steel tension rods or exposed beams—or beef up the remaining ties.

You can camouflage these structural changes behind finish materials or you can exploit them as design elements. (Your architect can help you work out details.)

If your attic is framed with trusses, your best bet is to leave the trusses in place. They, too, can be exploited architecturally; their bold, dynamic geometry can help dramatize the new space you are adding overhead.

Once you've worked out the structural and design details, you're ready to begin the actual work. Roll up (or bag up) the ceiling insulation and move any wires or ducts, if necessary. Then pull down the old ceiling and extend the wall framing into the attic. Run any new wiring called for in your plans, then insulate the new wall extensions and the underside of the roof. Staple a vapor barrier over the insulation and finish off the interior surfaces with drywall. *(continued)*

ANATOMY OF A RAFTER ROOF

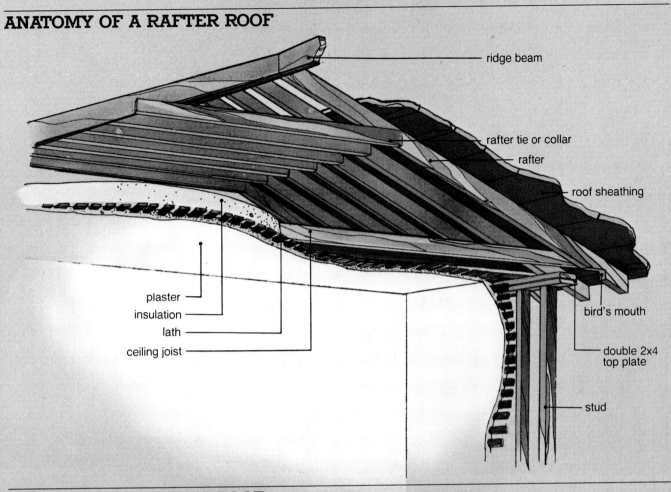

ridge beam

rafter tie or collar

rafter

roof sheathing

plaster

insulation

lath

ceiling joist

bird's mouth

double 2x4
top plate

stud

ANATOMY OF A TRUSS ROOF

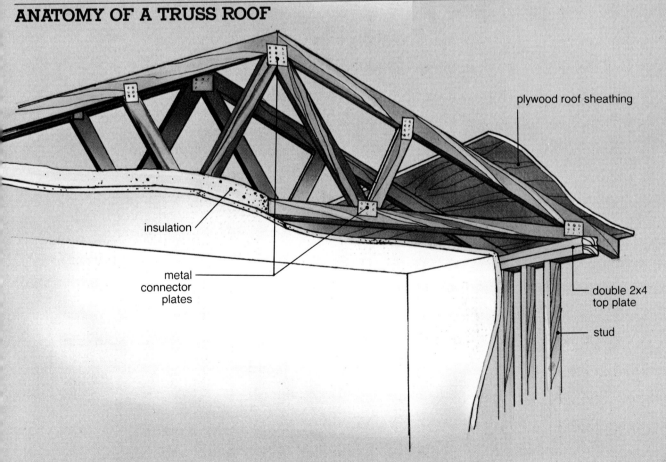

plywood roof sheathing

insulation

metal
connector
plates

double 2x4
top plate

stud

REACH UP
(continued)

After you discover how easy and inexpensive it is to create high-rise drama in boxy living spaces, you won't want to stop there. A whole new range of space-stretching ideas will unfold. If you're bumping the ceiling over a living room, for instance, you may find enough space there for that quiet adult retreat you've always wanted. If you're reaching up over a family room, you may be able to add a lofty playroom-dormitory for the children and convert downstairs bedrooms into extra space for grownups. Or you might have room to lift the ceiling over a master bedroom, turning it into a private two-level suite.

Finishing off an attic is an old space-stretching trick, but bumping up the ceiling as you go adds an interesting new twist: opening up between levels creates the illusion of endless, free-flowing space. As you wander from level to level, the rooms unfold gradually, not abruptly. Yet each area remains only partially revealed, so there's no need to sacrifice privacy.

Dramatic architectural effects also encourage you to use natural and artifical light more boldly. High walls and rakish ceiling planes become even more exciting when they're bathed in sunshine from a giant skylight or painted with overlapping circles of light and shadow from a row of track lights (see pages 38 and 39).

And you can create all this exciting interplay between levels without distorting the basic outlines of your house, so you need not give the exterior a face-lift unless you want to.

Bumping the ceiling: a lively conversion
For an example of this strategy in action, take a look at the dramatic interior pictured *right*. Originally, this space had about as much architectural appeal as the inside of a shoe box, and the attic above it was dark, dingy, and totally isolated physically and visually.

The homeowners swept away the shoe-box look by opening the main floor's ceiling and bringing the attic to life. The living room ceiling now soars to the top of the house and folds down behind a row of cantilevered bookcases into a loft-style sitting room. The sitting room itself, which forms part of a new upper-level master suite, provides a quiet perch for reading, watching television, or listening to music.

To avoid unnecessary expense, the owners left part of the structural system exposed and incorporated it into the design. Since the joists in the old ceiling had helped stabilize the roof framing, every third joist was left in place and beefed up with an extra framing member. This way, the other joists could be removed without weakening the system. Also, the edge of the loft was tied into the roof slope with angled cross bracing so the loft wouldn't need extra support across the opening to the dining area. In the peak above the loft, all the collar ties were left in place and concealed above a drywall ceiling.

Who's going to do the work?
As with removing a wall and installing a window, taking out a ceiling may or may not be a feasible do-it-yourself project— depending partly on your carpentry skills and partly on your family's willingness to live in a construction zone for an extended period of time.

The early, demolition stage can be fearfully messy, especially if your ceilings are plaster and lath. And if you have to add new structural members, you'll need a helper or two to lift them into place. If you do decide to take on all or part of the work yourself, consider renting scaffolding; it's a lot easier and safer than teetering at the top of high ladders.

(continued)

REACH UP
(continued)

Stuck with an attic you can't stand up in? Don't abandon it to cobwebs and dust quite yet. With some simple arithmetic you can put those idle cubic inches to good use. Just add the attic to the room underneath, then subtract enough headroom for a loft under the roof peak.

Since standard ceiling height in most rooms is 8 feet, you can "borrow" a foot or so and add it to the attic space without losing really essential headroom underneath. And opening the whole room up to the roof will more than compensate for a low-slung ceiling over one section.

You can apply this add-a-little/subtract-a-little formula in several different ways. For example, you could open up the attic over a bedroom, then tuck a loft under the roof for extra sleeping or study space. Or you could open up over the family room and build an upper-level work center for sewing, home planning, or moonlighting. Of course if your room already has a high sloping ceiling, all you have to do is add the loft itself.

To make the most of a split-level scheme, plan each area of the room carefully. If only part of the loft has stand-up space, devote the rest to sitting, sleeping, or storage. In turn, use the loft to define a similar area on the lower level. In a child's bedroom, for instance, you can tuck the sleeping area into the loft and set up a study space underneath, with built-in task lighting on the underside of the loft floor. Or you can perch the loft on top of a walk-in closet/dressing area or a specially designed play nook.

To avoid a chopped-up or over-structured look, concen-trate on basic shapes and simple, straightforward materials. And to preserve the sense of high-ceiling spaciousness, keep the design as airy as possible; bring in extra light through the walls or ceiling. Also, keep the furnishings simple—the bold outlines of the loft and the built-ins will serve very effectively as part of the decor.

A loft as a rewarding afterthought

The split-level bedroom pictured *left* demonstrates these principles nicely. Although you'd never guess it now, the loft was added after the room was built. It provides a quiet, out-of-the-way spot for a home office above the master bedroom.

The room had a cathedral ceiling to begin with, but the extra space overhead wasn't being used to best advantage, so the owners decided to reach up on one side above the sleeping area. Since the peak doesn't measure a full two stories high, they built the loft 6 feet 8 inches above the floor. This left plenty of headroom over the bed and allowed a clearance of 8½ feet in the loft.

The loft itself is supported on one side by a 4x12 beam and on the other by a 2x10 ledger anchored to the outside wall. Laminated wood decking, 2¼ inches thick, forms the loft floor and is nailed directly to the 2x10 ledger and to a second 2x10 bolted to the beam at the other side.

Open-tread stairs, flat white expanses, and simple wood trim make the room seem as spacious as ever; generous wraparound windows on both levels keep it bright and airy.

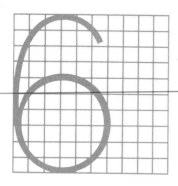

6

CONVERTING UNFINISHED AREAS

If yours is a family painfully in need of more living space, first look down, then up, then sideways. Basements, attics, and garages are the most popular ways to stretch a house that's pinching—and small wonder. Each offers "found" space that's yours for the finishing. This chapter tells how to assess the potential of these unfinished areas, advises how to deal with the special problems each presents, and gives examples of conversions that just may spark a new way of thinking about your house's possibilities.

As candidates for finishing school, basements have lots going for them. In most cases, heating, wiring, and plumbing are already there, along with enough square footage to fit in several rooms, or even an entire floor of new living. Unless yours is an older home with only a separate exterior stairway, access isn't a big problem. And if your budget is tight, you can probably do all or most of a basement finishing job.

But before you rush out to order the materials for a conversion, consider some of the difficulties you may have to overcome. Water problems can render belowground space uninhabitable. Ceilings may be uncomfortably low. And unless yours is a walk-out basement, it probably receives very little natural light.

All of these problems are surmountable (the following pages offer solutions), but any one of them might suggest that you look at other unfinished areas first.

From basement to tavern
If you decide to go underground, by all means let your imagination loose when you develop a design theme. The owners of the home shown *opposite*—a 120-year-old with a stone foundation—chose to re-create a colonial tavern, complete with barn-board paneling, details that replicate period workmanship, and an open-hearth fireplace. First, they carpeted and partially enclosed an interior staircase. Next, they partitioned off two major spaces: a sitting area and a bar (see plan *below*).

The fireplace, *opposite above*, replaces an outside cellar entrance. After installing a new concrete foundation for the hearth, the owners studded out the wall behind, covered the studs with fire-resistant wallboard, then followed up with a layer of twisted and bent metal lath. To this they applied a thick coat of perlite plaster that melds the fireplace and the stone walls around it.

The bar area *opposite below* demonstrates that a windowless space need not be dark and cheerless. Shutters, lit from behind, give the illusion of windows and compensate for the room's lack of the real thing. *(continued)*

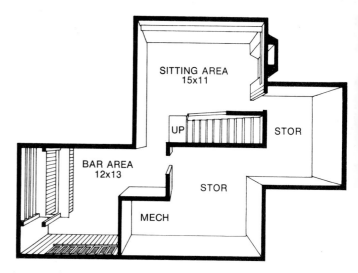

BASEMENTS

(continued)

DAMP-PROOFING WALLS AND FLOORS

If your basement has moisture problems, you first need to determine how water is getting in. Here are the main possibilities and what to do about them.

• *Condensation.* Damp walls, dripping pipes, and mildew may indicate simple condensation. To find out, tape a piece of foil to the wall. If the room side of the foil is coated with tiny droplets of water after a few days, condensation is the culprit. A new, insulated inner wall will solve this problem.

• *Seepage.* If you find water on the wall side of the foil, suspect that moisture is seeping through the wall surface. A couple of coats of waterproofing masonry paint will stop seepage.

• *Leaks.* Cracks and holes that ooze small amounts of water usually can be plugged by forcing waterproof hydraulic cement into them, then sealing with masonry paint. If you can actually see water flowing

through the walls, you may have to attack the problem from outside by rerouting downspouts, by regrading fill next to the foundation, or by digging down to the footings, installing drain tiles, and waterproofing the walls of the foundation.

• *Damp concrete floors.* Overcome these by anchoring nailing strips to the floor, then cover everything with a polyethylene vapor barrier, and top off with sub- and finish flooring, as illustrated on page 107.

FINISHING OFF CEILINGS

If yours is like most unfinished basement ceilings, it probably includes a maze of framing members, pipes, heating ducts, and other not-so-nice-to-look-at elements. How can you best cover all that clutter?

The answer depends mainly on how much headroom you have down here, so start your analysis by taking a few measurements. First measure from the floor to the bottom of the joists overhead; this, minus a few inches for floor and ceiling materials, will be the highest point of your ceiling. Next note how many pipes, ducts, and other obstructions drop below the joists; these will establish your lowest ceiling levels.

Now let's look at the three main ways to go:

• *Acoustic tiles* are the most popular. They subtract only a

few inches from your maximum headroom and are easy to piece around obstructions that run below joist level. The 12x12-inch tiles go up quickly, but you first have to install furring strips to the undersides of joists. Furring a ceiling can be a time-consuming process.

• *A suspended ceiling,* such as the one in the shop shown *opposite,* goes up much more quickly. You simply hang a grid of special metal channels from wires, then set 2x4-foot panels into the grid. The main drawback of a suspended ceiling is that it must drop at least 3

inches below your *minimum* ceiling level (so you can set the panels in place); most basements don't have enough space for this.

• *A drywall ceiling* like the one above the study shown *opposite* gives a basement all the finish and polish of upstairs space. But drywalling a ceiling and taping the joints between panels is tricky—sometimes arduous—work, especially if you must piece around obstructions. If you want a smooth, unbroken drywall ceiling in your basement, consider hiring a professional for this phase of the remodeling.

One other option is to simply forget about finishing your ceiling and leave everything exposed. Pages 94 and 95 show a remodeling where this ploy worked well.

Because they're below-ground, isolated from other parts of the house and from the outside world, basements make especially good spaces for get-away-from-it-all activities. If your leisure-time pursuit demands peace and quiet—or makes so much noise that it drives other members of the family to distraction—maybe you should claim a corner for your own.

The photos here show two different ways to go. This shop, *opposite top,* is a handyman's dream with ample storage and work surfaces. It also serves as a complete family crafts center capable of handling several different activities at once. Or maybe you'd prefer a parents-only retreat where you can relax with a book or catch up on paper work; if so, check out the study pictured *opposite below.*

Planning a workshop

Examine the shop's plan, *opposite top,* and you can see it measures just 12x16 feet, so every square inch had to be put to good use. Workbenches line up against two walls, leaving the center of the room free. When it's not in use, a table saw mounted on casters rolls into a special niche under one bench. Pegboard and open shelving keep tools handy, without taking up the space that bulky, closed cabinets would have occupied.

Just about any work space can benefit from a sink, such

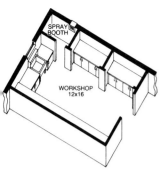

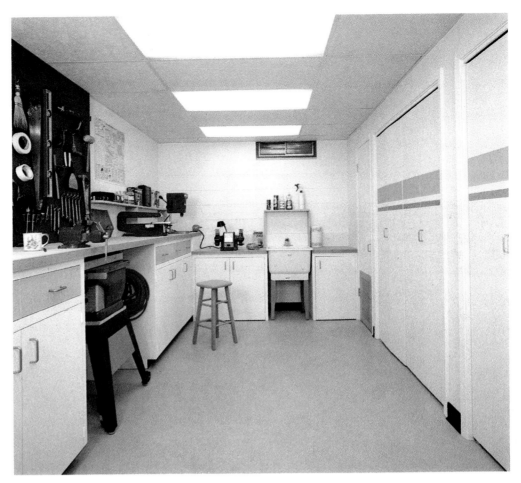

as the laundry tub against the far wall. To simplify the hook-up, try to position it as close as possible to existing plumbing lines.

A pair of craft centers, concealed behind double doors, make this shop especially noteworthy. Though not much larger than a closet, each center includes a counter, shelves, and lighting. Open the doors, pull up a stool, and you can work in comfort. And instead of having to clean up in the middle of a project, you can leave everything as is, turn off the light, and close the doors.

A third small room (see plan) serves for spray painting. Louvers in the door and an exhaust fan in the basement's outside wall dispel harmful fumes from paint.

Fitting out a basement study

The combination study and home office occupy half of a basement; the other half includes a play/family room (see plan *below*).

The twin desks here consist of a length of laminated-plastic counter top installed atop ordinary two-drawer file cabinets. Above the desks, shelving and cubby-holes organize books, correspondence, office supplies, and memorabilia. A painted valance up top hides hardware that suspends the shelves from the ceiling.

(continued)

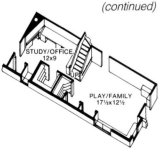

BASEMENTS
(continued)

How's the headroom in your basement? If your ceiling is less than 7 feet high, you'll have to either lower the floor or raise the house. Clearly, jacking up an entire house is an expensive, risky proposition. But with time, muscle, and tools, you can drop the floor level enough to make basement space usable for living areas.

The multi-level remodeling shown here is a case in point. Originally the basement ceiling measured only 5½ feet high. Two months of grueling work that involved everyone in the family (see box *at lower right*) lowered the floor 2 feet.

Once the earth was removed, the family tackled the problem of connecting their excavated space with the rest of the house. They accomplished this by removing a section of the floor above, and by building a 3x12-foot extension that runs from the old basement floor level up to the roof line (see plans *below*).

The two-story-high space, *right*, now serves as a new entry/planning area, and accommodates a curving stairway that rises to the kitchen. Three steps down is a 26x15-foot recreation room.

The view from the recreation room, *opposite,* shows just how successful the project turned out. About all that's left of the old cobwebbed cellar are the joists overhead. These remained exposed to increase height, and to contrast with the smooth surfaces of drywall and ceramic tile.

Beyond the window and grilles in the background you see another benefit that resulted from the remodeling. A new patio, surrounded by a privacy fence, provides outdoor living and a welcoming approach to the new front entry.

What about footings?
Excavating more than a few inches below basement floor level could undermine the foundation of your home, so seek the advice of a masonry contractor before you begin work. The contractor may suggest something like the solution used here—low concrete-block retaining walls just inside the perimeter walls to shore up the home's footings. These are concealed under counters and behind built-in seating. You also may need a soil survey to ascertain that digging won't dip into the water table underneath.

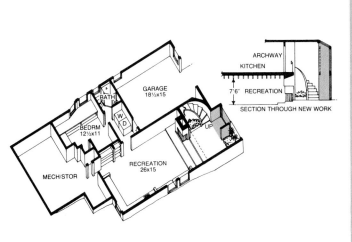

GARAGE 18½x15

BATH

BEDRM 12½x11

W D

MECH/STOR

RECREATION 26x15

UP

ARCHWAY
KITCHEN
7'6" RECREATION

SECTION THROUGH NEW WORK

DIGGING IN

The biggest impediment to digging out a basement is that most earth-moving machinery won't fit down there. This means the work has to be done by hand, a shovelful at a time.

If you can, hire a crew for the pick-and-shovel phase. If not, prepare for an arduous task.

Excavation for this remodeling began when the family's 13-year-old son attacked the old concrete floor with a sledge hammer and crowbar. The family then constructed ramps and wheelbarrowed the debris and earth outside. As dirt piled up, anyone with free time loaded it into a pickup truck for hauling to the dump. Finally, after establishing the new floor level, the family poured a new concrete floor.

Would they do it again? "We couldn't have done it at all if we had to pay for labor," said one member of the family. "But today we would probably hire out the heavy work."

ATTICS

As potential new living spaces, attics entice with two easy-to-get qualities: light and ventilation. Your attic may be shy of these now, but envision how it would be with added or enlarged gable windows. Add a dormer, and still more light and fresh air enter the picture. Your attic can go from a dark tomb to a bright, breezy room—if it measures up.

Nothing short of raising the entire roof will create headroom that's just not there to start with, so begin your assessment by measuring from the attic floor to the ridge beam that runs along the peak of your roof. Anything less than 10 feet will cramp an attic's potential for new living space.

Now give thought to how you're going to get up there. If you already have a stairway with adequate headroom, access shouldn't be a problem—unless, of course, you want to change the location of the stairway. If you don't already have any easy way to the attic, you'll have to add a set of stairs (see the box on page 98 for help with this planning).

Next, get in touch with an architect, builder, or a local building official who can tell you whether the existing floor will support new living space. In some houses attic joists are sized and spaced the same as regular floor joists. Usually, however, attic joists are designed solely to support the ceiling below them. If that's the case, you'll have to add or beef up joists before you can install finish flooring.

If you want to make a dramatic difference in the way the attic space looks, your next step may be to install a dormer like the one shown *above* and in the drawing *opposite*.

A dormer brings more than just a treetop view; it also adds extra headroom and helps diminish the cramped feeling that steeply sloped ceilings create. Adding a dormer certainly isn't a job for a beginner (see box, *opposite),* but knowing what's involved will enable you to talk knowledgeably with contractors.

Running heating, air conditioning, and electricity to the attic is the next step; these may be jobs you can do yourself. If so, be sure to have your work inspected and approved by local officials. If the ductwork and wiring are to go behind walls, have the inspection done before you install drywall or paneling.

When your dormer is in place and services are run, the bulk of the difficult conversion work is over. Much of what remains is a job anyone handy with a hammer and saw can handle successfully.

You must install insulation in attic walls and ceiling. In most cases, simply cut fiber glass insulation to fit between roof rafters and gable end studs. If the insulation doesn't have a vapor barrier attached to it already, install one over the insulation. You can finish interior surfaces with drywall or paneling. Installing these materials on sloped surfaces requires patience and muscle, but the basic procedures are fairly straightforward. Detailed house-building and renovation books can show you how this is done.

To assess your attic's potential, study the examples on the next few pages; you'll see how each remodeling job has solved problems unique to its own situation. *(continued)*

ANATOMY OF A DORMER

Dormers can be framed in either of two different ways—shed-style, such as the one shown here, or gable. Gable dormers have two sloping roofs that meet at a ridge running perpendicular to the main roof ridge. Of the two types of dormers, a shed style usually provides more room; however, add the type that will better harmonize with the overall appearance of your house.

Both are constructed in much the same way. First shingles and sheathing are removed from the roof area the new dormer will cover. Next the rafters on either side of the cut are braced so the roof won't sag. Once the intervening rafters are cut, their free ends are tied together with a *header* up top.

In most instances, the bottom of the dormer rests on the *top plate* of the exterior wall below; this is a doubled 2x4 that also supports the lower end of roof rafters.

The dormer's side walls are supported by the existing rafters; its roof ties into the newly installed header and rests on a second header installed atop the dormer's rectangular window wall.

As you can see, dormer framing can be tricky. It also has to be done swiftly, so your home's interior is exposed to the elements for as short a time as possible. With careful planning, skilled carpenters can frame a dormer and sheath its exterior surfaces in a day or two.

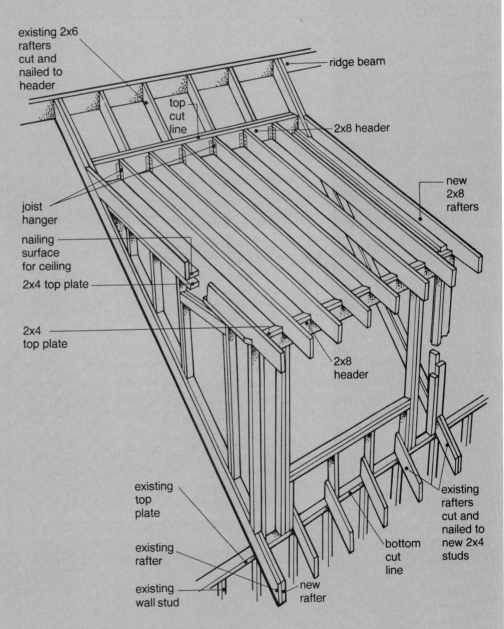

existing 2x6 rafters cut and nailed to header

ridge beam

top cut line

2x8 header

new 2x8 rafters

joist hanger

nailing surface for ceiling

2x4 top plate

2x4 top plate

2x8 header

existing top plate

existing rafter

existing wall stud

new rafter

bottom cut line

existing rafters cut and nailed to new 2x4 studs

ATTICS
(continued)

GAINING ACCESS

If the current route to your attic is nothing more than a ceiling hatch, you'll have to install a stairway—and this means giving up some space on the floor below. Allow at least a 3x10-foot rectangle for a standard staircase, a 5½-foot square for circular stairs.

Where your stairway goes depends not just on the floor space available, but also on the headroom you'll have above the stairs. This should be at least 78 inches from step to roof at any point along the rise. For this reason you'll probably want the stairway to go directly under the roof ridge. If this isn't feasible, plan stairs so they run parallel to the roof's slope and end up as close to the center of the attic as possible.

In searching for access to your attic, first consider space above any existing stairways. If that won't work, look for a centrally located closet that shares a wall with a hallway. As a last resort you may have to steal a few square feet from the largest or least-used room on the level immediately underneath.

The owners of this story-and-a-half bungalow nearly doubled their living space by finishing off the attic. Economical construction-grade 2x4s create a framework that both beautifies and solidifies the new room.

To avoid a clutter of tiny rooms, the floor plan is completely open, providing a sitting area, home office, and master bedroom all in one space. Separated only by the stairway, chimney, a new fireplace, and stall-style partitions, areas merge under the dramatic sweep of the new framing members.

The challenge in any attic-finishing project is to make efficient use of low space under the eaves. Here the bed, desk, seating, and storage line the perimeter, leaving most of the floor area open. To further conserve space and money, a colorful rug covers the closet.

The stairway, *above,* demonstrates yet another way the

owners saved money. Attic flooring, removed to make way for the stairway, was recycled as paneling for the stairway walls and risers.

Another innovation helps conserve heating costs. By removing a section of floor along the attic's southernmost edge (behind the seating at far right, *opposite),* the owners took advantage of natural convection currents from the level below. Sun-warmed air rises to help heat the new room.

(continued)

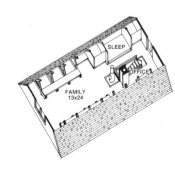

This lively bedroom/playroom area was carved out of the attic of a 55-year-old house. About one-third of the attic space was left for storage; the 700 square feet that remain now are nifty nooks and crannies for the family's two boys.

The room's cozy niches came about naturally, thanks to dormers and a drywall ceiling that follows the existing rafter line. Whether sleeping, studying, or reading, the brothers can coexist in one large space without sacrificing personal privacy.

A variety of built-ins—from simple platforms to sturdy desks—runs along the perimeter of the space. Each boy has his own storage areas, which minimizes disputes about what belongs to whom.

With no vertical walls, standard windows were out of the question. Instead, the owners installed several skylights that flood the room with sunshine. (The box *opposite* explains what's involved in adding a skylight.) Besides providing illumination, these skylights open to work with pre-existing windows in providing excellent cross-ventilation.

Carpeting that covers the entire floor minimized the need for new furnishings. Just a few fluffy pillows turn a simple low platform into a comfortable reading area. The carpeting also reduces noise transmitted from the attic playroom to living quarters below.

Sleeping and study areas are at opposite ends of the space; each child can sleep or study without disturbing the other. (For another view of this attic conversion, see pages 16 and 17.) *(continued)*

ANATOMY OF A SKYLIGHT

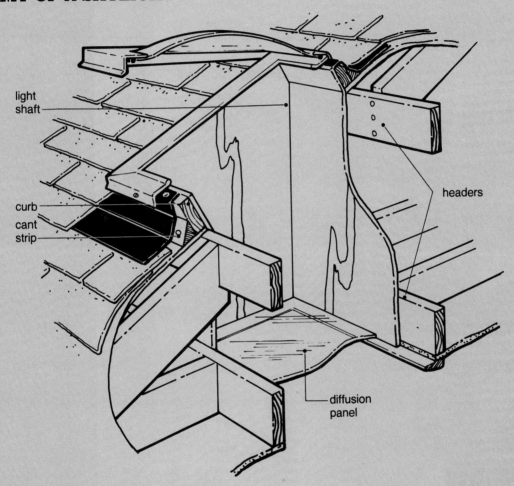

light shaft

curb

cant strip

headers

diffusion panel

A skylight, whether fixed or operable, offers one of the simplest, most dramatic ways to bring light to a dark attic. If you're a moderately skilled carpenter and not afraid of heights, you could do the work yourself; most manufacturers include step-by-step installation directions with their units.

The job usually starts with removing shingles and sheathing from the existing roof. Next, one or more rafters are cut and their free ends tied together with 2x6- or 2x8-inch *headers*.

Instead of installing the skylight directly on the roof, most manufacturers recommend that you build a *curb* to prevent water leakage. This is nothing more than a simple wooden frame built atop a roof and sealed to it.

After the curb is in place, mount the skylight securely on top of it. A *cant strip* around the base of the curb helps seal the finished skylight structure and directs water away from the curb.

If your roof and the ceiling of your new attic room are separated by dark, unused attic space, you may have to carry the installation one step further with a *light shaft*. A light shaft directs illumination from the skylight down into the room. Generally, the sides of the light shaft are painted white and a *diffusion panel* is installed at the room opening to distribute light as much as possible throughout a room.

When you select a skylight, keep energy efficiency in mind; double or triple glazing helps to prevent heat loss. Operable units, which cost more than fixed ones, help dissipate heat buildup that occurs in summertime.

The remodeled attic shown here began as a typical cobweb collector. Skillful planning transformed it into a bedroom/den/bath suite that functions as a self-contained, away-from-it-all retreat for parents.

The metamorphosis began with a careful sizing up of the situation. Dark and tunnel-like, the space had dinky windows at each gable end and a series of massive collar beams that tied together the rafters overhead.

Dividing the attic into three separate yet interrelated rooms went a long way toward solving the proportion problem. Leaving the beams in their natural state and accentuating

them with a painted drywall ceiling added strong horizontals that "square-up" this angular space.

The floor plan, *above*, shows how double doors lead to a bedroom at one end, a bath at the other. Strategically placed skylights bring light into the den area. One skylight directly over the stairway keeps the stairs safely illuminated during daylight hours; another located above the double desk sheds genuine moonlight on moonlighting projects.

Here again, seating, work, and storage places line up at the edges of the room, where low knee walls would make stand-up activities impossible.

INSULATING ATTIC SPACES

One of the big appeals of an attic-finishing project is that it offers an excellent opportunity to upgrade your home's insulation. Do a proper job of bundling up the top of a house and the energy savings work their way down to the rooms below.

If your attic currently has any insulation at all, it's probably under the floor. Clearly this isn't going to do anything to cut heat losses and gains through the roof, so you'll want to either relocate existing insulation or simply buy

new material and install it between the rafters.

When you shop for insulation, pay close attention to R-values, which are the measure of a material's resistance to heat flow. The higher the R-value, the greater the insulation level.

You'll also discover that insulation comes in a variety of different forms, each suitable for a particular application. Here are the types:

- *Batts* of fiber glass or rock wool are 4- to 8-foot-long strips that fit between rafters and floor joists. Because you simply lay them in place, they make especially good sense in difficult-to-reach locations such as the spaces behind knee walls.
- *Blankets* resemble batts but come in continuous strips with flanges that can be stapled to framing members. They're easily installed between rafters.
- *Loose-fill* insulation comes in bags and can be poured

Both photos show the view from the stairway. White surfaces and restrained colors bounce illumination throughout the space, making the 15½x20-foot room seem larger than it actually is.

What are your options for attic space?

Just because your attic has enough headroom, easy access, and the other criteria we've already discussed doesn't mean it's the ideal candidate for future development. You must answer one more important question: What would you like to do with the new living space?

If, for example, you plan to do a lot of large-scale entertaining, an attic probably would make a less-than-ideal party room. Your guests won't appreciate trudging upstairs, and you won't have much fun running up and down to answer the door or refill snack bowls.

Even certain types of quiet zones are unsuited to attic space. Many of us are entranced by the romance and self-sufficiency of heating with a fireplace or wood stove. But lugging wood all the way up to the attic—and ashes back down—can be a back-breaking way to save on fuel bills. This doesn't mean you shouldn't consider a wood-burning unit at the top of the house; just don't count on it as your only source of heat there.

A bedroom, study, or other personal area probably makes the best use of attic space. If you do decide on sleeping quarters, consider making the investment involved in extending plumbing up there, too. A new bath isn't cheap, but it pays off in convenience every day you use your new living space. Also, it usually will add to your home's resale value.

or blown with a special machine into cavities you couldn't otherwise reach, such as the crannies out at the ends of eaves where rafters and joists meet.
• *Foam* materials make most sense for already-finished walls and ceilings and must be installed by professionals. The contractor makes a series of holes in surfaces, then injects foam into stud and rafter cavities to provide the needed insulation.
• *Rigid* insulation consists of boards of foam-like plastic. It's more expensive than other types, but has a higher R-value per inch of thickness. Some rigid insulation emits toxic vapors when ignited, so fire codes often specify that it be covered with drywall, even if you plan to put up paneling as a finish material.

Regardless of the type you choose, you'll want to install insulation in any wall or ceiling that doesn't have heated space on the other side. To prevent condensation within walls and ceilings you also need to include a *vapor barrier* of paper, foil, or plastic sheeting between the insulation and heated living spaces. Some insulation materials come with a vapor barrier attached; with others, however, you must staple a separate membrane to studs or joists.

Finally, don't forget about insulating windows and skylights. Double- or, in some climates, triple-glazing is a must. Insulated shutters or draperies further reduce energy leaks.

If your house has an attached garage or carport, you've probably already begun to wonder whether that space could be put to better use as finished living quarters. Footings, a roof, and several exterior walls—the most costly elements of an addition—are already in place. At most houses the garage is close to an activity zone such as a kitchen. And because everything is aboveground, plenty of natural light is available.

Perhaps best of all, the architecture of your garage or carport probably harmonizes with your home's exterior, so you have no complicated design problems to solve. Who would guess, for example, that the new wing shown here once sheltered the kitchen and a three-sided carport? When the owners wanted a family room, they simply closed in the opening with a new fireplace, French doors, and clerestory windows, *above near right*. The family cars weren't completely evicted, either; they now nestle into a new carport that adjoins the old carport.

Sizing up your ceiling possibilities

One early problem you'll face in converting a garage regards the height of the ceiling in your new living space. Garages are typically framed with 7-foot-high wall studs, a height that would be uncomfortably low for a ceiling. So, many remodelers choose to top off their new living space with a cathedral ceiling like the one shown *opposite*. Here, space between the rafters was insulated with rigid foam boards, then finished off with drywall and stucco-like texture paint.

If you prefer a more conventional look, consider insulating with fiber glass blankets and installing a suspended ceiling hung 6 inches to 1 foot above the tops of the wall studs. Suspended ceilings, which come in kit form with complete instructions, are surprisingly easy to put up.

In fact, other than heating, wiring, and plumbing work, most of the tasks involved in finishing off garage space require only limited skills and can be accomplished as a series of weekend projects. The mess won't interfere with everyday living, so you can take the time for a professional-quality job. *(continued)*

INSULATING AND HEATING YOUR GARAGE

Since most garages and carports have bare stud walls inside, insulating them is a simple matter. Just staple up batts or blankets, taking care that you get a snug fit and leave no voids that could result in wasted energy dollars. If the insulation doesn't have a vapor barrier, cover it with polyethylene to protect against condensation.

The drawing here shows how paneled walls typically go together, but check your community's building code before putting up paneling. Some codes require that you first install a layer of fire-retardant drywall.

You'll probably want to insulate the floor, too. See the box on page 107.

For heating you have two choices: either extend existing ductwork or install an independent heat source, such as a through-the-wall furnace or electric baseboards, that you can regulate separately.

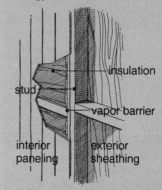

insulation

stud

vapor barrier

interior paneling

exterior sheathing

Finishing off a garage poses one big interior design problem: how do you keep the new space from looking like what it once was?

The garden room shown here offers several solutions. First, instead of simply walling up the old garage door opening, the owners installed four big glass panels. Then they opened up the rear and side walls with more windows, and augmented natural lighting still further with a series of skylights. Lots of light and leafy views in all directions dispel any out-in-the-garage feeling. Windowsills, 9 inches deep and topped off with ceramic tile, create a waterproof base for potted plants that give the indoors an outdoor quality.

NEW FLOORING

Concrete may be fine for a car's tires, but it's not the most comfortable surface for human feet. To give yourself a warm footing, top off the old concrete with an insulated floor.

First repair any unsound sections of the old floor. Then call in an exterminator to spray a long-term pesticide along any perimeter cracks. Seal the entire floor with a vapor barrier of polyethylene sheeting held down with dabs of roofing cement.

Next install a perimeter sill of 2x4s (one or more stacked so the finished floor will be at or near the level of floors in the house). Fasten the sills with lead expansion anchors and lag bolts every 16 to 20 inches, leveling the sills before tightening the bolts.

Next come "nailers," 2-inch or thicker nailing strips attached to the concrete on 12-inch centers and toe-nailed to the sills. Insulation, either batts or loose-fill, goes between the nailers.

After the wall framing is complete, nail a subfloor of 3/4-inch plywood to the nailers. Your choice of finish flooring tops off the job. If wiring, plumbing, or ductwork is to go under the floor, position it before nailing on the subfloor.

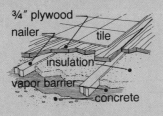

To cut the cost of fixed windows in a project like this, look for panels of insulated glass that are sold as replacements for sliding glass doors. Installing at least one set of sliders that open helps ventilation and makes for easy indoor-outdoor living during warm months.

Another difficulty with both one- and two-car garage spaces is their basically boxy shape. Examine the lower photograph, *opposite,* and you can see how one small structural change gave this room an entirely different look. The owners simply removed a section of the wall between garage and house and connected their new garden room with the front entry foyer. Now only a change in levels separates the two spaces.

If you decide to remove all or part of a dividing wall, be warned you'll most likely be tampering with an important structural element—a wall that helps hold up your house. Seek a contractor's advice about the bracing you'll need. As an alternative, consider simply removing the connecting door between the house and garage.

Other uses for garage space

Because of its usual proximity to the kitchen, a garage makes a strong candidate for that family room you may need—but it can also be adapted for other areas. Let's look at a few of the possibilities.
- *A new bedroom.* A small, two-bedroom house with a single-car garage could easily gain a third sleeping space. And if kitchen plumbing is nearby, you might include a new bath as well. With about 10x20 feet of space to work with, the bath could go at one end of the space, the bedroom at the other.
- *A home office.* Consider evicting the car and converting its quarters into a studio or office. This might make special sense if your business attracts visitors because clients can come and go without disturbing family activities. Caution: check zoning regulations first; some laws prohibit business enterprises—especially those that generate lots of traffic—in residential neighborhoods.
- *Work or hobby space.* Need a shop, darkroom, home gym, or other special-purpose room? Again, an attached garage may offer a way to go. Unusual conversions such as these might detract from the salability of your house, but with ingenuity you could keep construction costs to a minimum and perhaps even plan changes that could be easily removed if you decide to sell.

Dividing a garage

If you live in a cold climate and don't relish the thought of clearing ice and snow from your car on winter mornings, consider going just halfway by converting only a portion of a two-car garage. To shelter a single automobile, you need no less than 10x20 feet. For most two-car garages, this leaves about the same amount of space for new living space. In many cases you won't even have to reroute the driveway. Just replace the double door with a single and build a new wall down the center.

Once again, check building codes before you begin. Most require that any wall between garage and living space be built with extra fire-resistance. Gasoline is highly flammable and explosive, and you don't want to jeopardize your family's safety or nullify insurance coverage for a disaster that might result from an illegal conversion.

Complying with codes

Speaking of codes, it's a good idea to check any conversion plan with your community's building officials before you begin. Some stipulate that you'll need a building permit and inspections of the changes you'll be making. Making your plans a matter of record could lead to a reassessment of your property value, but that's a small price to pay compared with the costly headaches that could otherwise result from an illegal conversion.

(continued)

Most two-car garages have at least 400 square feet of floor space—plenty of room for a cozy apartment. The conversion shown here packs in a living room, a sleeping alcove, a bathroom, and a kitchenette, all in space that was once a 17½x22-foot garage and an adjoining utility shed.

Before embarking on a project such as this one, check with your local zoning office to ensure that your proposed conversion complies with regulations; residential zoning often prohibits two-family dwellings.

Most of this conversion is devoted to a conversation area, *opposite*. A freestanding fireplace and exterior siding recycled into wainscoting defines this living area nicely.

Sleeping platforms stand directly behind the wicker sofa, *right*. In the loft above the bed, a second mattress serves as a study area, or accommodates overnight guests. Behind both beds runs an L-shape walk-in closet.

The kitchenette and bath (out of camera range to the left of the sleeping platforms) went in what was once an 8½-foot-wide storage shed that ran the length of one garage wall. Instead of tearing out the entire wall between the shed and the garage, the owners created a large archway connecting the kitchenette and the living area. This separates the two areas yet keeps them open to each other for easy access.

A sewer line and plumbing, electricity, and natural gas lines were extended to the apartment from the main house, about 25 feet away.

Obviously, a garage attached to a house would make an even simpler conversion than this one did.

Most impressive in this change from garage to apartment is the atmosphere of the new living space; it gives no hint that it once sheltered two cars. Further, the open plan relieves the cramped feeling of small partitioned areas.

A wise selection of finish materials often is critical, as was the case here. The ceiling, of tongue-and-groove knotty pine, presents the perfect foil to the space-enlarging white-on-white walls and trim work; and the old concrete floor springs to the step under newly laid carpet (in the living areas) and Mexican ceramic tile in the kitchenette.

Adding several large windows completely banished a garage-like feeling from the apartment. In many instances, windows offer an expeditious means of filling in old garage doors (see box *at right*). Here additional windows in other walls help brighten the space.

One final point about garage conversions: the outside walls support the entire roof structure. Interior partitions, therefore, do not have to bear loads, which greatly simplifies any remodeling job. So if you'd like a conversion you can carry out yourself, look to your garage. *(continued)*

CLOSING IN THE DOOR

Closing in a garage door needn't be difficult. Start by removing the old door and its trim and track mechanism. Next, construct a standard stud wall frame (2x4s or 2x6s spaced 16 inches on center). Build the frame on the garage floor and then tip it into place; nail the top plate to the old door's header and nail or bolt the bottom plate to the garage floor. Finally, sheathe and side the completed frame, fill it with insulation, and finish the inside with drywall. The drawing shows some of the details of framing a window.

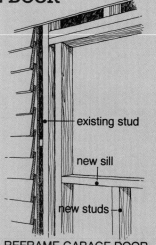

existing stud

new sill

new studs

REFRAME GARAGE DOOR OPENING TO ACCEPT WINDOW

An attached garage converts easily to living space because the house and garage already share at least one wall. When the garage is detached, or attached only by a breezeway, you have to work a little harder—but the results can be just as satisfying.

The remodeling shown here was created from a narrow breezeway and a double-wide single car garage (see plan). Enlarging the breezeway and adding a narrow bath/laundry corridor to the garage space helped integrate the new studio with the existing house. The refurbished garage screens a private deck and includes a wide-open workroom. A snappy-blue ladder leads to a 2½-foot-deep storage loft. In the bath corridor, vertical blinds provide needed privacy.

A fully detached garage presents problems of its own, especially if you want to connect to the house. If the house is close by, you'll have to build a corridor or a full room from the ground up. Of course, all this new construction—along with the expense of bringing in heat, electricity, and possibly plumbing—sharply increases the cost of converting a detached garage. If the house and garage are widely separated, consider converting to a function that can stand alone— a poolside bath house, for instance, or a guest apartment. A simple walkway might be all you'll need to connect with the new living space.

If the examples of garage conversions in this chapter make your heart beat a little faster, it's time to size up your own garage's potential. The box *below* will help you decide whether converting the garage is a practical solution for your space needs.

BEFORE   **AFTER**

GARAGE
24½x26

DECK

BATH

STUDY/OFFICE
24½x26

LIBRARY
12x24

SIZING UP YOUR GARAGE'S POTENTIAL

If you've decided that you need your garage more for people than for cars, ask yourself these questions:
• Is your garage structurally sound? If not, a brand-new addition may be more economical than a conversion.
• What would finishing the garage do for your home's floor plan? For example, how will you get to and from the new space?
• Can you extend your present heating and wiring systems? Can plumbing go in at a reasonable cost?
• Will you have room elsewhere for a car? Converting only a portion of the garage may solve this problem; adding a carport is another option.
• Will building codes in your community conflict with your plans?

If you get satisfactory answers to these questions, contact an architect or contractor. Even if you expect to handle most of the design and building yourself, a professional's advice will ensure that you are on the right track. The professional might even point out a better or less costly way to accomplish your goals.

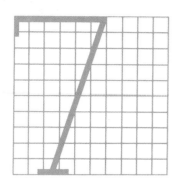

PUSHING OUT

Yet another way to stretch living space is to let out your home's belt a notch or two by expanding its exterior boundaries. Of course, you could do this with a major addition. But at today's prices, the foundation, roofing, and other construction costs might well rival (or even exceed) what you paid for the house in the first place. This chapter explores a couple of more economical ways to go: closing in a porch and bumping out a wall with a bay, greenhouse, or mini-addition.

CLOSING IN A PORCH

The owners of this home had no place in their kitchen where two adults and three children could sit down together for a meal. Obviously they needed more space. They got it—rather cheaply—by closing in an adjacent screened porch. Now the family has not one, but two eating areas: a counter where a wall once separated the porch and the kitchen, and a sunny breakfast room in what once was a porch.

What's more, the breakfast room, with its large expanse of glass, lets the family enjoy the outdoors much more than the old porch did—in any kind of weather. Windows along the bottom crank open for cross ventilation; Roman shades screen out hot sun and minimize nighttime heat losses.

Closing in a porch doesn't require building from scratch. But you may have to strengthen the foundation, build up and level off the floor, and add sturdier wall supports. You'll certainly need to construct a few new exterior walls (and insulate them, the floor, and the ceiling). Before beginning, check to see whether you must obtain a building permit.

(continued)

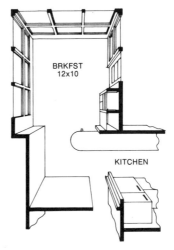

CLOSING IN
A PORCH
(continued)

If a porch is also a front entry it bears a special social responsibility: it introduces the rest of the house and makes guests feel welcome. These two closed-in front porches used to welcome guests about as effectively as a limp handshake. Now they warmly embrace newcomers in a way that says, "You're special, and we're glad to have you here." But note how differently each does it.

Large double-pane windows along the southern frontage of this enclosed porch, left and above, let winter sunlight strike the floor, which serves as a thermal mass. At night the floor releases its heat to warm adjoining rooms. Eye-level windows open to admit breezes; an overhang helps shade the windows during the warm months when the sun travels higher in the sky.

W arren Harding conducted a presidential campaign from his front porch, and millions of Americans used to devote leisure hours to "jes' sittin' " and watching the neighbors pass by. Campaigning has changed since then, and so have the habits of most families. Nowadays, all too many front porches have simply outlived their usefulness.

This was the case at both of the older homes shown here. Now innovatively enclosed, each not only stretches living space, but also serves as a passive solar collector that helps lighten the heating load.

The bungalow, *left,* dates back to Harding's time, and originally had an open porch framed by massive piers. To enclose it, the owners simply filled in the spaces with a combination of fixed and operable windows and several linear feet of new walls. The old piers were painted white and covered on the outside with cedar siding stained light gray; inside, the original brick wall was clad with the same siding applied diagonally to add visual interest. Now a king-size entry, this former porch also serves as a comfortable family lounge and overflow space for party guests congregating in the adjacent living room.

This little Victorian cottage, *right,* sacrificed none of its period charm when the small front porch was closed in. The conversion includes a wide fiber-glass skylight up top and a combination of fixed glass and fiber glass along the south-facing front. Inside, an array of greenery and a cozy hammock greet guests.

(continued)

Here, at left and above, aggregate on the floor serves as thermal mass, storing heat during the daytime and releasing it at night. In the ceiling a vent, not pictured, conducts heat to second-floor rooms; openable windows at both ends of the former porch carry off unwanted warm-weather heat.

CLOSING IN
A PORCH
(continued)

Old-fashioned sleeping porches are rare today. But if you're lucky enough to have one, you have the makings of an exceptional all-weather room. Here a sleeping porch began life anew as a master bedroom with space for more than just sleeping. The room just as easily could have become two average-size bedrooms, a studio, solarium, or hobby room. The beauty of this conversion is that it loses none of its original advantages as a sleeping porch—the new room still enjoys a treetop view of the woodsy backyard and gathers in plenty of sunlight and fresh air.

When the owners of this comfortable two-story decided to add a master bedroom, they knew instantly where to put it—in a seldom-used sleeping porch that spans the rear of the house. They didn't even need all the space for sleeping, so they converted half into an area for reading and relaxing.

Best of all, the project wasn't costly. The major expense was for windows that went on top of the parapet walls where screening used to be. The ceiling dropped a few inches to make room for new insulation; drywall replaced the old shingles on the walls; plywood subflooring went smoothly over the original tar-paper floor before hardwood strip flooring went down. Except for painting, that's basically all there was to it.

You could probably handle a job like this, but a contractor would likely finish it faster.

Light and neutral shades in paint, furniture, and accessories give this room an airy, open feeling. Blinds roll all the way up to flood the room with strong light, and let down to filter glare. The small, step-out balcony, a pleasant holdover, provides a canopy over the ground-level back door.

BUMPING OUT
WITH A BAY
OR GREENHOUSE

Most of us shrink from doing anything to a house that will alter any of its structural components. Remove part of an outside wall? Never. Even drilling a tiny hole for the TV antenna wire gives us the willies. But fortunately not all bump-outs require structural alterations. For some, you simply buy prefabricated units, which come in many shapes and sizes, put them together, and install them in existing window openings. Prefabs perform every bit as well as customized units do, and you don't have a hole in your house for several days.

To find out which bump-out will fit your situation, ask yourself what you want the bump-out to do. Do you want a better view of the backyard, or an architectural accent to dress up the exterior of your house? Should it contain lots of storage space, or include just enough extra room to display a few plants and collectibles? Do the windows have to open, or will fixed glass do? If you want openable windows, do you prefer double-hung or casement types? How important is insulation? (If you live in a widely variable climate, you'll need double-pane glass to reduce heat transfer.)

Once you've determined, at least generally, what you want, measure the area where you want to put the bump-out. It might just cover an existing window, or it could be bigger. Whichever you decide, make sure you have all your measurements with you before looking around.

You may have to visit several building suppliers or home improvement centers to find what you're looking for. Some units will be in stock; others you'll have to look at in manufacturers' catalogs. If the dealer doesn't have literature for you to take home, write down specifications and make rough drawings in a notebook.

The bump-out pictured here is on the lower end of the cost scale. This and similar ones cost less than $500 and come in kits. The parts simply slip together; you don't even need a screwdriver to complete the assembly. (But you will need one to mount it.) You can fasten the unit directly to the exterior wall, but it's better to build a wooden framework, attach it to the house, then screw the assembled unit to the frame.

Serious home horticulturists often buy larger, more elaborate greenhouses, rather than the bump-outs shown here, and attach them to one side of the house. These are made of double-insulated glass that's tinted, tempered, and sometimes curved. The smallest protrude about 3 feet from the house, measure 10 or 12 feet in length and cost about $2,500 installed, not including flooring or foundation. For the same kind of unit in the jumbo size—15 feet long, approximately 10 feet high—you'll spend around $14,000, exclusive of foundation and heating. Architectural bump-outs—bow and angle-bay windows—also present a wide range of sizes as well as styles. They range from about 4 to 13 feet long; prices from about $700 to $2,500, uninstalled.

(continued)

In this prefab bump-out, the screw holes in the metal parts are predrilled, so you need only take a quarter-inch drill and make a few guide holes in the frame for the wood screws. Because the unit cantilevers from the house, you don't need expensive foundation work.

BUMPING OUT WITH A BAY OR GREENHOUSE
(continued)

Many projects never get past the thinking stage. By the time we've figured out all that could go wrong and have puzzled over the minor details of execution, we've talked ourselves out of the job. Prefab bump-outs such as the unit shown on pages 118 and 119 offer one way to get past this hurdle—but custom-builts can be almost as easy for you or a contractor to pull off. The key is to cantilever out from your home's structure, which eliminates any need for expensive, laborious foundation work. Here are a couple of "for instances."

Both of the bump-outs shown here began as ordinary windows that opened and closed but that did little else. To push out, the owners simply removed the windows and constructed glass boxes in their places.

The mini-greenhouse, *opposite* and *bottom right,* consists of simple platforms at its top and bottom, with three sheets of acrylic plastic in between. Fish-tank silicone sealer joins the panels to each other and to the house.

Though it projects only 18 inches, this bump-out must be strong enough to support not only plants but also any person who might step out onto it. Support came from splicing extensions onto the home's floor joists, which, of course, ran perpendicular to the wall.

The buffet bump-out, *upper* and *center right,* required a bit more framing expertise. Here, also, joists were extended. Then the contractor added conventional exterior walls; installed a big pane of fixed glass and two standard, crank-operated casements; and constructed cabinetry inside. Diagonal bracing adds strength to the 2-foot-deep structure.

If the floor joists at your house run parallel to the window you'd like to push out from, don't give up hope. You may be able to hang a unit like this one from the eaves and simply bolt to the sill. An experienced carpenter can tell whether this ploy will work in your situation. *(continued)*

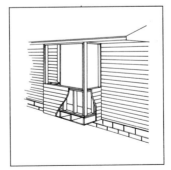

The bump-out above and left provides a kitchen eating area with much-needed serving and storage space, plus an expanded view of the greenery outside. The cutaway drawing shows how it was framed.

Removing a double-hung window and dropping its opening to the floor made way for the sunny planter left and opposite. With the wall opened up, the room seldom needs artificial light during the day.

BUMPING OUT
WITH A BAY
OR GREENHOUSE
(continued)

The two greenhouses you see on these pages have almost nothing in common. One is small and unobtrusive; the other room-size and impossible to miss. You could build the smaller one yourself in a day or two for a few hundred dollars; the other would require the services of a contractor, several days of work, and several times the money. Despite these differences, the two greenhouses have one important thing in common: they both stretch existing space into something new and imaginative.

The compact greenhouse, *left,* not only provides a nicely sized, attractively designed spot for plants, but also solves a couple of problems in the bargain. The greenhouse area was once a front entry that was visually humdrum and that directed incoming traffic right into the middle of the living room. The owners decided to solve both problems simultaneously by relocating the entry and giving its old location over to their collection of plants.

Because the area faced directly onto the street, however, they had to figure out a way to preserve their privacy without shutting off too much light. Their solution was to build the greenhouse's front wall from exterior-grade cedar and to install glass for the end walls and the roof.

Their strategy worked perfectly. The greenhouse enjoys privacy from the street yet admits plenty of light for the flora within. The greenhouse is 7 feet long, 9 feet at its peak, and extends 3½ feet from the wall—not spectacularly large, but certainly up to the task it was designed for.

Instead of removing the old concrete stoop, the owners left it right where it was as a splash-proof floor for the greenhouse. Another bonus: the stoop already was pitched to allow water to run off.

Look closely at the exterior view, top, and you'll see how panels at the bottom sides of the greenhouse open for cross ventilation during warm weather; screens keep out insects. Inside, bottom, a wall across the bottom of the greenhouse hides unattractive pots.

Here again, the owners were able to make use of an existing floor, this one of broken brick, shown in the interior view, right. The exterior photo, bottom, shows how the greenhouse snuggles between house and garage, and opens to an existing terrace.

This greenhouse, *right,* didn't really bump out anything: instead it filled in a do-nothing breezeway between the house and the garage. Two of the walls already existed, so the major part of the project consisted of erecting a glass canopy, putting up one new wall, and installing a couple of sliding glass doors.

The canopy presented less of a problem than you might think. It's a standard-size commercial unit ordered through a dealer and put together at the site. In the model shown, the top panels open manually when a cord attached to pulleys is pulled; but the same unit also comes with a motorized opener hooked to a thermostat. When the greenhouse gets too warm, the top panels open automatically, then close when the temperature drops to a preset level.

The canopy is supported by 2x4s nailed horizontally across the outside walls of the house and garage. The beams across the top of the greenhouse appear to be providing support, but their primary function is aesthetic. They also can be used to suspend hanging plants and things such as wind chimes.

This greenhouse is in Atlanta, Georgia, where the owners report it requires no supplementary heating, even during the coldest months of the year. In colder climates, the greenhouse would need a heater of some kind.

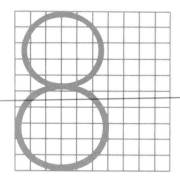

START FRESH WITH A WHOLE-HOUSE REMODELING

Not so many years ago, when you tired of a house or outgrew it, you simply sold out and bought another. "Trading up" was almost a national pastime. But things have changed quickly. Now, few people can afford to play musical houses because of rising construction costs and mortgage interest rates. More people are staying put these days. In a way they're still "trading up," but now it's different. They're taking the house they live in and—with a full-scale remodeling—turning it into the house they want. In this chapter you'll learn how you, too, can keep the same address but have a new house.

Undertaking a whole-house remodeling demands careful planning, and still more careful planning. Tearing your house apart and putting it back together again is a big, costly, and complex task. You'll need all the resources you can muster to pull it off successfully.

First and foremost is your plan of attack—not the actual blueprints or drawings; these come later. By plan of attack, we mean your overall approach to the project: what you want to do to your house; who will do it; when, where, and how it will be done; and how you'll pay for it all.

Start by analyzing your goals and needs. What do you want your house to have that it lacks now? Put everything down on paper no matter how petty or preposterous some items may seem. An intercom system, a whirlpool in the master bath, a greenhouse off the kitchen, an extra bedroom over the garage. Now's the time to inventory your dreams; later you can decide what's reasonable—and affordable.

Start a file
Start sketching and collecting pictures and plans from magazines, books, and other sources. Not that you'll want to copy other ideas exactly, but they can serve as a valuable source of inspiration for your ideas, as can remodeling projects of friends and neighbors.

Your plan of attack is very apt to involve at least one addition. If so, you'll have to decide where it will go and how it will attach to and harmonize with the rest of the house. Will your lot have room for an addition without infringing on your neighbor's property or compromising your privacy? Consider, also, the effects on your energy needs.

An addition on a house's south side might almost heat itself by catching the sun's rays with large expanses of glass or a solar collector for heating water. If your addition has to go on the north side of the house, design it with but a few small windows—or none at all.

Get expert help
Even if you're proficient at home remodeling, you'll likely need the services of a contractor, and maybe those of an architect or designer as well. Do you know how to get good guidance? More about this on pages 126 and 127.

As you formulate your plan of attack, decide what work you're going to do yourself. How much time can you really spare? Which steps in the process can you perform skillfully, and which should you leave to professionals?

All plans of attack must also account for inconvenience. Your house will be in a shambles for several weeks or months—maybe even longer. Can you put up with a mess underfoot and workers in your house all day, or possibly do without the use of several rooms at one time? If not, look at the alternatives: boarding in a hotel or an apartment—expensive, of course—or at the neighbors' while the house is under siege.

Finally, can you afford to remodel? You may have to borrow money. Is your credit good? Banking relationships strong? Will an extra monthly payment strain your ability to meet existing expenses?

Obviously, a whole-house remodeling gives you a lot to think about, but if you take the time to plan carefully, the odds weigh heavily in your favor. And you'll end up enjoying your house as never before.

WORKING WITH A CONTRACTOR

Finding a good contractor and establishing an effective working relationship is a little bit like courtship and marriage. First you have to make a good match, then you have to live with the person.

You wouldn't look for a mate in the Yellow Pages, and that's not the place to seek a contractor, either. A listing, even a large display ad, says absolutely nothing about workmanship and integrity—the two most important qualities you need in a contractor.

Instead, talk to friends, neighbors, and business acquaintances who have contracted for remodeling. Were they satisfied with the quality of the work? Did the contractor finish the job on time and with a minimum of prodding? Was the contractor neat, easy to work with, dependable, open to suggestions? Above all, did the contractor stay within the budget agreed upon?

Solicit recommendations until you have at least three. Then look at work each contractor has done. Invite each to discuss the job you have in mind. If any of your prospects strikes you as uncommunicative, moody, overbearing, or otherwise objectionable, scratch this candidate from your list.

Determine, too, whether each contractor is used to doing the sort of work you want done. The home shown here, for example, started out as an "urban basket case." The owners chose to maintain its exterior character, *upper right,* yet open up its interior, *opposite,* for a contemporary flow of spaces. They needed—and found—a contractor skilled at both restoration and large-scale interior remodeling.

When you talk with a contractor, also find out whether he's bonded, insured, and covered by workmen's compensation. If not, you could be held financially liable for workers' injuries on your property. Likewise, check bank references, your local Better Business Bureau, and the Consumer Protection Agency to see whether anyone has filed a complaint against a contractor you are considering.

Soliciting bids
Once you've identified at least three likely contractors, ask for written, detailed bids from each. Make sure that each contractor is bidding on *exactly the same project,* right down to the last beam, panel, and fixture. Here, the burden is on you and your architect (if you have one) to assure that specifications are complete and can't be misinterpreted.

When all the bids are in, you're ready to make a choice. You'll be tempted to pick the lowest, of course, but be suspicious if it's substantially below any of the others. Maybe the contractor has overlooked something big, or "low-balled" his bid in a desperate attempt to get the job. Either way the contractor will have to make up for the disparity later—by cutting corners in workmanship and materials, or by asking for more money.

Neither, in most cases, should you select the highest bid unless the price is only slightly high and the bidder has an outstanding reputation for good work and reliability.

Coming to terms
The contract you and the winning bidder sign should spell out in plain language all elements of the job, including

detailed specifications, a guarantee of the work (ideally for at least five years), and a completion date. The last should be followed by the words: *time is of the essence.* If litigation occurs, your seriousness on this point will be assured. Get the starting date in writing, too.

Similarly, the contract should bind the contractor to complete all components of the job *in a workmanlike manner.* This means simply that the contractor must do the job right. Again, this is for your legal protection.

Any contract you make should spell out the schedule of payment as well. Some contractors may try to collect a hefty down payment up front; resist them. A reasonable and commonly used formula calls for one-third when you sign the

contract, another third when the work is substantially advanced, the last third when the work is completed.

Finally, as the job progresses, you or the contractor may feel that an element needs different handling. Regardless of whose idea the change is, be sure to get the new cost *in writing* before you give your go-ahead.

UPPER LEVEL
BEFORE

AFTER

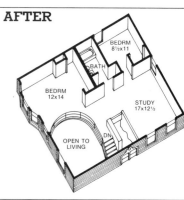

MAIN LEVEL
BEFORE

AFTER

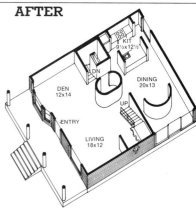

START FRESH
WITH A
WHOLE-HOUSE
REMODELING

**DOING ALL
OR PART OF
THE WORK
YOURSELF**

BEFORE **AFTER**

Remodeling can be a "them or us" proposition. You can hire a contractor to do the whole thing—that's the "them" approach. Or you can take the "us" approach and do all the work yourself (providing you have the skills, of course). But ofttimes the best approach is to combine both "them *and* us." You do as much as your time and talents allow, and let the contractor do the rest. You keep control of the project, and your budget, leaving the hard stuff to the professionals.

The owners of this home are professional designers, and the job they did on their small, boxy old house gives ample proof of their talents. Originally the house offered little more than "possibilities," which is exactly what the owners wanted when they bought it.

They planned to do most of the work themselves, and their combined backgrounds as designers, coupled with outstanding home-remodeling talents, easily qualified them for the task. At the same time, they knew their limitations and they wisely decided to hire a contractor for two tricky and time-consuming jobs—pouring a foundation and building the exterior shell for the new kitchen.

That's the kitchen jutting out the left side of the house in the exterior photo, *below.* The owners also added a greenhouse and deck just in front of the kitchen, and relocated the main entry (yellow door) where once were some windows in a little-used porch.

To appreciate their achievement, first examine the before and after plans, *above,* then

the photo of the living room, *opposite,* which gives the view as you look toward the stairs and beyond to the new greenhouse.

To open up space here, the designers removed a wall that split off a cramped hallway and also eliminated a closet under the stairway. The old, deteriorated ceiling came down, too, exposing joists that provide a mellowing constrast to stark, white walls. A storage divider provides bonus wall space for arranging furniture.

Assess your talents and time

The owners knew what they could and couldn't do, or at least what they would or wouldn't do. It often is difficult to understand the difference if you've never undergone a whole-house remodeling, but

extremely important that you try. Botched or badly done remodeling only can have a negative effect on the value, function, and appearance of your house, and blunders in structural and electrical work pose serious safety hazards. So know your limitations and work within them.

Remember, too, that most remodeling jobs take longer than anyone—your contractor or you—anticipates. This means you'll need plenty of staying power when it comes to completing jobs that take a lot of time. If you're already working 40 or more hours a week at your job, entertaining on weekends, and doing volunteer work in the evenings, you'd better think twice about undertaking any kind of long-term remodeling project on your own. *(continued)*

DOING ALL
OR PART OF
THE WORK
YOURSELF

(continued)

Another reason growing numbers of people are taking on whole-house remodelings has to do with the "new" popularity of city neighborhoods. Here's where you can still find homes close to schools, shopping, night life, maybe even within walking distance of work. Prices often are surprisingly affordable, and some cities offer loans at below-market interest rates.

The photos and plans here provide a good example of what a turn-of-the-century city house can become. From the backyard garden, *above,* you can see how big new windows bring light into a once-dark interior. Inside, *opposite,* walls came down to open up boxy rooms.

Who's going to do what?

If you aspire to urban pioneering, we won't even try to dissuade you from attempting to breathe new life into an old house. We will, however, offer some suggestions about which jobs you can take on yourself and which are better hired out.
● *Excavating.* Unless you have access to heavy machinery and know how to operate it, digging out for even a small foundation could take weeks of hard labor—work a contractor could do in a day or two.
● *Plumbing.* Plumbing jobs fall into two general categories—supply and drain lines. With patience and a how-to-do-it book in hand, most amateurs can modify supply lines or even replace an entire system. Drain work can be arduous and tricky, however, especially

if you need to add or replace a main soil stack.
● *Wiring.* Most electrical jobs are simpler than they seem, provided you learn to work safely and follow local codes. If a house needs new electrical service from the street, hire a professional to bring it in and install a new service panel.
● *Drywalling.* Here economies of scale determine who should do the work. If you have only a modest amount of drywall to install, by all means do it yourself. But for bigger projects, a contractor possibly can do the job cheaper than you can; with quantity discounts and scaffolding and other specialized equipment, a contractor often can buy and install a room's worth of drywall for less than it would cost you just to buy it— and in much less time.
● *Stripping woodwork, painting, papering, paneling, and minor demolition.* These are all basically unskilled, labor-intensive jobs you're best off doing yourself. Not only do you save money, you also get exactly the results that you planned for.
● *Any job that needs doing quickly and without interruption.* Tearing off a roof, pouring a sizable concrete slab, or remodeling a room the family will use extensively are examples of work you can ill afford *not* to contract for.

SIZING UP OLDER HOUSES

Before you make an offer for an old house, have an architect or structural engineer give it a thorough inspection. Here are some of the things the architect (and you) should look at:
● *Settlement.* Sight down the sides of the house to make sure outer walls are plumb and square. If they're not, the house is structurally unsound and not worth remodeling.
● *Sturdiness.* Jump in the center of rooms to check for springy floors. These could indicate sagging joists and beams; they can be shored up, but the work is expensive.
● *Termites.* Poking structural members with a screwdriver can tell you whether insects are at work inside. If they are, pass up the house.
● *Moisture.* Leaky roofing is replaceable, but if it has leaked for years, water may

have done considerable damage inside. Look for stains, peeling paint, and falling plaster, especially on ceilings. If damage is in just a few areas, it is repairable, but you will want to budget for this.
● *Plumbing.* With most older homes you can just about count on having to replace water supply lines, so concentrate on drains, especially the main soil stack. Find an exposed section and whack it hard with the handle of a screwdriver. A clear ring indicates the stack is okay; a dull sound means it needs replacing, an expensive but not impossible proposition.
● *Wiring.* Unless the home was rewired in the past 30 years, you should budget for a complete electrical overhaul.

MAIN LEVEL
BEFORE   AFTER

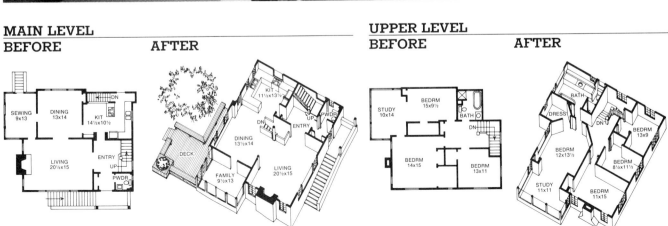

UPPER LEVEL
BEFORE   AFTER

FINANCING A MAJOR REMODELING

As we've warned, pulling off a whole-house remodeling calls for patience, planning, creativity, and hard work. Finding the money for a project this big poses similar challenges. First you have to locate a source for the funds you need, then you have to strike a deal that suits your circumstances.

Lending institutions are accustomed to writing mortgages for new or existing homes. The property itself serves as security so the lender's risk is low.

The value of a remodeling, on the other hand, lies more in the future. How the job turns out—and even whether it's completed at all—greatly affects the lender's security and increases the risk. This is why you may discover that a number of institutions are flatly not interested in loaning money for a whole-house remodeling.

Others will, however, and with persistence you can track them down. Here are five possibilities for funds. (Caution: times change, and lending laws vary from state to state. Use this survey and the chart opposite only as starting points in your quest for remodeling money, then research the specifics.)

Government-backed loans

Let's say you're thinking about becoming an urban pioneer. You've found a run-down house in a deteriorated neighborhood that seems on its way back up again. You'd like to buy the house and immediately remodel it.

With a government-backed loan you may be able to get enough money to buy the house *and* pay for the remodeling. Guarantees from federal, state, or local governments (or a combination of government loans) make it possible for a lender to provide funds at less than the going interest rate, and often with a low down payment as well.

If the neighborhood turns around as anticipated, you could end up with a home whose market value greatly exceeds the total of your initial investment plus improvements; if not, you might be stuck in an undesirable area with an oddball that's difficult to sell.

The availability of government-backed loans varies widely from year to year, city to city, and even area to area within cities. Predictably most involve red tape for you and for the lender, and many limit eligibility to low-income families. Still, if your family and neighborhood qualify, you may be able to get financial help for a whole-house remodeling.

Construction loans

Another way to borrow for a purchase/remodeling situation involves a financial two-step: you obtain a mortgage to buy the home based on its value as is, and take out a construction loan to pay for the remodeling. Construction loans are risky and always go for a higher rate of interest than permanent loans, so you'll want to engineer in advance an arrangement that lets you refinance at your home's total improved value after your project is complete.

Construction loans can be complicated. You may have to deal with two different lenders —one for the property loan, another for the construction loan; periodic inspections may be required to assure that the work is being done properly; and the sooner you can complete the remodeling, the sooner your monthly payments will decrease.

A second mortgage

If you already have substantial equity in your home, or if you're buying and can persuade the seller to "take back paper" by helping to finance the purchase, a second mortgage may offer a way to finance a big remodeling job.

Second mortgages pose a higher risk than do first mortgages for lenders (they're not first in line if you default), so interest rates typically run two to five percentage points above prevailing rates. Terms are usually shorter than those for first mortgages, too—from five to 15 years—which means you may have to shoulder some hefty monthly payments on top of what you're paying against your present mortgage.

You might negotiate a rate more favorable than you can get from a lending institution— though probably not a longer term—if the seller will give you a second mortgage. Sometimes called a "purchase money" mortgage, this arrangement can appeal to an owner eager to unburden a slow-moving property. Laws regulating private mortgages vary from state to state, and any financing deal between a buyer and seller should be examined by a lawyer—so proceed with caution if you choose to go this way.

Life insurance and retirement trusts

"Whole" life insurance policies and some employer retirement funds, trusts, and savings and investment plans build up a cash value you can borrow against. Interest rates are generally low. You pledge a part of your policy or trust as collateral, reducing your coverage until you pay off the loan.

Home-improvement loans

Home-improvement loans, which rarely exceed $10,000, make sense for a small project, or for a big remodeling you're planning to accomplish in stages. Because improvement loans require less paper work than construction loans or second mortgages, more lenders are willing to consider them. But the trouble with stringing out two or more improvement loans is that you have to pay off one construction stage before you can begin the next stage of a protracted project.

Getting the money

Loans against insurance policies and retirement trusts are easy to obtain; you simply fill out a form and wait for the check. Home-improvement loans don't usually entail a lot of paper work, either. But the other sources discussed here require that you make a well-thought-out presentation to the lender. Here's what it should include:

● Specifications that give detailed descriptions of everything you intend to do. These should be approved by a licensed engineer, contractor, or architect.
● Plans showing all changes. You'll also need these when you file for a building permit.
● Bids from a contractor or subcontractors that verify what labor and materials will cost for each job you intend to do.
● Comparable sales prices for improved and unimproved homes in your neighborhood. A realtor can usually provide this information.
● If you plan to rent out any part of the property, an accountant's cash flow statement should spell out how income from the rental will help pay back your loan.

SOURCES FOR REMODELING MONEY

	ADVANTAGES	DISADVANTAGES	AVAILABILITY
GOVERNMENT-BACKED LOANS	Lower interest rates and package deals that combine money to buy a home with funds for a whole-house remodeling. You make a low initial investment and gamble that the neighborhood will improve.	Typically limited to rehab situations in bad neighborhoods. Many stipulate restrictions on income.	Highly dependent on public funding for loan programs. Some lenders don't like to bother with government-backed loans.
CONSTRUCTION LOANS	You obtain the money to finance a remodeling, then pay it out in three or four stages as work is completed. Afterward, you refinance with a conventional mortgage.	High interest rates mean you'll be making sizable monthly payments while your remodeling is in progress—and the longer a job drags on, the more you pay in total loan costs.	Lenders are accustomed to dealing with builders, developers, and other large-account customers; many won't bother with homeowners. A good presentation of your situation and needs is imperative.
SECOND MORTGAGES	A way to tap some of your home's equity without refinancing the total amount. A second mortgage may be used to pay off a construction loan when the remodeling is finished.	Interest rates may be two to five percent higher than first mortgages are costing. Terms are shorter.	Many lending institutions prefer to avoid second mortgages. In times when conventional mortgages are expensive or hard to get, owners anxious to sell might be persuaded to consider lending to a buyer.
LIFE INSURANCE AND RETIREMENT TRUSTS	Interest rates lower than any of the other sources. Involve no red tape.	The coverage of an insurance policy is reduced by the amount you borrow; with trusts, the loaned portion doesn't grow in value.	Most straight life policies let you borrow against cash value; check with your employer to learn whether you can borrow from your company's trust fund.
HOME-IMPROVEMENT LOANS	A fairly simple way to go, especially if you'll be drawing out the project by doing all or most of the work yourself.	Upper limits on what institutions will lend are often well below the price of a whole-house remodeling.	Banks, savings and loan associations, and credit unions are often eager to lend to customers or members who have good credit ratings.

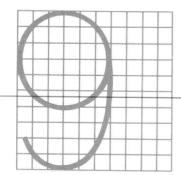

MAKING THE MOST OF YOUR HOUSEHOLD BUDGET

If anything around most homes is tighter than space, it's money. The preceding chapters show how to enjoy more living in the space you have. This chapter tells how to get more value out of the dollars available. First priority, of course, is to establish a budget and learn to live within it. In this chapter we'll help you develop a workable budget plan, which will put you in a good position to come to grips with the costs of owning a home. Then, we explain how you can project what any home improvements would do to the resale value of your home.

If you've been budgeting by the seat of your pants, or following a plan that's out of date, now's the time to get out a pencil, pad, and calculator. What you're after is a financial overview realistically based on income and outgo, but not bogged down in nickel-and-dime details.

Also incorporate future goals in this budget and make it flexible enough to adapt to changing circumstances.

Here's a four-step program that tells how to get started. Use the table on the facing page as a model to create your own method of recording and reviewing your cash flow on a monthly basis.

First, what are you spending?
Get all records together, including all receipts, check stubs, and last year's tax return. Now sort expenses into three categories: fixed, occasional, and variable.

Fixed expenses remain the same from month to month and must be paid each month. Mortgage payments (except variable ones), rent, and installment loans are typical fixed expenses. Occasional expenses occur with some regularity, but not monthly—insurance premiums, tuition, some utility costs, taxes, and the like.

Variable expenses include outlays for items such as restaurant tabs, clothing, bank card bills, house operating outlays, automobile upkeep, and food costs.

Once you have all records and estimates in hand, figure yearly totals for each category, then divide by 12 to get a monthly average. You may notice that the records leave something to be desired. If so, resolve to do better at keeping receipts and noting the pur-

poses of checks, especially any written for cash. One solution, carry a notebook to itemize out-of-pocket expenses. These are a common source of budget problems.

Second, establish goals
Your primary aim is to live within your means; but saving and investing should be an integral part of your budget goals, too. These goals typically fall into three categories:
• *Emergency cash*. Most financial advisers recommend that you have the equivalent of three to six months' take-home pay in a savings account that allows easy, quick withdrawal of funds without penalty.
• *Short-term goals*. These are anything you plan to pay for within the next year or so. Try to put these funds into a savings instrument that pays high interest and matures at the time you'll need the money.
• *Long-term goals*. These might include a down payment for a new house, college tuition, or retirement funds. Shoot for the highest possible return on investment during the time period you're considering.

Third, set up your budget
Project a plan for the year, using the averages from the past 12 months, any out-of-pocket expenses, plus any increases, such as higher taxes or insurance premiums, that you know are coming. Make a separate chart for each month, plugging in projected income and expenses now and actual data at the end of the month.
• *Income* includes salaries, dividends, interest, and anything else the Internal Revenue Service says is income.
• *Savings*. List all savings under fixed expenses.
• *Occasional expenses*. Allot one-twelfth of the projected annual total for each month of

TRACKING MONTHLY EXPENSES

MONTH _____

	PROJECTED	ACTUAL		PROJECTED	ACTUAL		PROJECTED	ACTUAL
FIXED EXPENSES			**VARIABLE EXPENSES**			**MONTHLY INCOME**		
Rent/mortgage	$_____	$_____	Groceries	$_____	$_____	Take-home pay	$_____	$_____
Personal loans			Meals out			Spouse's take-home pay		
Car loans			Household operations			Social security		
Installment loans			Gas or oil			Bonuses		
Savings/investments			Electric			Tax rebates		
Alimony/child care			Telephone			Interest income		
			Water and sewer			Dividend income		
Total fixed expenses			Maintenance			Rental income		
			Other			Other		
OCCASIONAL EXPENSES			Home furnishings					
(figure annually and divide by 12)			Transportation			Total monthly income		
Insurance			Gas and oil					
Life*	$_____	$_____	Car repairs					
Health*			Public transport					
Car*			Other			**YOUR MONTHLY PLAN**		
Homeowner's*			Clothing					
Other*			Cleaning, laundry					
Taxes			Medical and dental not paid by insurance			Total income	$_____	$_____
Property*			Personal care items			Total expenses		
Income*			Credit card and charge accounts			Fixed		
Other*			Entertainment			Occasional		
Tuition/camp*			Pocket money			Variable		
Vacation			Contributions, dues					
Other			Misc. job expenses			Income minus expenses		
			Other					
Total occasional expenses			Total variable expenses			*actual due date and full amount		

---

the year. Before shopping, review outstanding bills. This may help curb impulse purchases.
• *Allow for inflation* by factoring in an additional percentage for items that periodically rise in cost. Base your percentage on the last two or three increases.

Finally, review and adjust
Each completed chart will show a net gain or loss for the month. If a deficit results several months in succession, you'll obviously have to cut your spending. Here are a few ways to do it:
• If credit payments (excluding mortgage) exceed 10 to 12 percent of your take-home pay, stop using credit until you drop below that level.
• Look for specifics, such as long distance phone charges or entertainment expenses, that come in consistently higher than projected. Either cut back, or increase the amounts budgeted and cut elsewhere.
• Reexamine priorities. You may find that you can save for *either* a washer and dryer *or* a vacation, but not both.
• Sharpen shopping skills. Look for sales, save coupons, learn to drive a hard bargain.
• Conserve energy to reduce heating and cooling costs.
• Make savings automatic with automatic paycheck deductions or monthly transfers from checking to savings.
• Take advantage of professional financial counseling offered by credit unions and banks. For information on nonprofit consumer credit counseling services, write: National Foundation for Consumer Credit, 1819 H Street NW, Washington, DC 20006.

MAKING THE MOST OF YOUR HOUSEHOLD BUDGET

HOW MUCH DOES YOUR HOME REALLY COST?

In most family budgets, shelter constitutes one of the largest single expenses. Do you have an accurate picture of what it costs to keep a roof overhead? You have the mortgage payment, of course, along with other monthly costs, such as utilities. Then you have additional outlays for taxes, insurance, maintenance, and repairs. Here's how to account for all these items in your budget plan.

Perhaps you'd really rather not know what it costs to run a house, but to budget accurately you have no other choice. Many of these costs are beyond your control, but if you pin them down now and accurately forecast how much they're likely to rise, you'll be in a good position to plan the financial future of your family.

One way to keep a running tab on home-ownership expenses is to set up a file folder for each category and fill it with receipts as you pay your bills. If you haven't been doing this, conduct a search of your check register and other relevant sources. Here are the categories you'll want to monitor.

Mortgage

Many homeowners remit real estate taxes to the bank along with their monthly mortgage payment. If your lender requires this, separate the loan payment from the amount of the tax. (The bank's notice may do this; if not, ask for a breakdown.) If insurance is also included, deduct that amount, too. Once you've divided up the elements that made up the total amount sent to the bank each month, write down each on a separate line. Why bother doing this? Because if your monthly payment goes up, you'll know right away which element is the culprit.

If yours is an older, fixed-rate mortgage, that part of your payment won't change unless you refinance or take out a second mortgage for some reason. If yours is a variable-rate mortgage, you'll have to do some forecasting. Will it go up? How much and when? Some variable-rate mortgages can be adjusted only once every one, two, or three years; others rise and fall more frequently according to economic indicators.

Taxes

You can almost count on it that property taxes will go up. Again the questions are how much and when. Community newspapers usually forecast increases as the cost of services rises. If a tax hike is in the wind, project it in your budget.

Other than taking an active political role, you can't do much about the *rate* at which your home is taxed. You can, however, appeal any changes in its *assessed valuation*. Appeal procedures aren't difficult, but you have to prepare your case carefully. A successful appeal should result in a reduction of current taxes, and establish a fairer basis for future assessments.

Insurance

Not all insurance companies provide the same coverage at the same price. Here's one category where it can pay to shop around, especially if you've just received a notice about an increase. Poll neighbors and friends about their insurance costs. If you suspect you're paying more than necessary, talk to several agents and get competitive bids.

While you're at it, review your coverage. Are you adequately protected? You'll pay more for increased coverage, of course, but any claims could be reduced if you've under-valued your home.

Maintenance and repairs

This is the most elusive category to track, but also the one most directly under your control. Receipts and check stubs can tell where money went for major items, but how about cash payments? Does the neighbor child charge $5 or $8 to cut the lawn, and how many times was it cut? How much money went for hardware-store and garden-center items?

Little things paid for in cash can add up quickly, so it's a good idea to keep track of them in a notebook, or save receipts—no matter how small—in a file.

Knowing what your maintenance and repair costs amount to also offers a way to minimize them. If, for instance, you discover you're paying a plumber for periodic visits to clear a chronically stopped-up drain, you might save money in the long run by either buying your own power drain auger and doing the job yourself, or replacing the old drain with a more efficient one.

Utilities

Home energy costs continue to rise, and there doesn't seem to be much any of us can do about them. We can, however, put brakes on the amount of energy we consume. Turning off unnecessary lights, adding more attic insulation, investing in storm windows or other energy-saving devices can all save dollars, or at least minimize the effect of rate increases.

Cash flow can also be a crippling aspect of utility costs. Some suppliers offer budget plans that spread your estimated annual cost evenly over 12 months. If your utility doesn't have such a plan, consider setting aside money during times of the year when costs are lower. This, along with the interest it has earned, could help balance your budget during peak months.

TRACKING OWNERSHIP COSTS

	PRESENT	PROJECTED	SPECIAL NOTES
MORTGAGE	To get a true figure, be sure to deduct any tax payments and insurance premiums.	Fixed-rate mortgages remain the same; older variable-rate mortgages sometimes include a ceiling on interest rates; newer mortgages may be pegged to the prime rate and change monthly.	Another way to look at the true cost of mortgage payments is to factor in the savings you gain by deducting interest from your taxable income. Multiply the interest paid by the rate for your tax bracket.
TAXES	If your bank collects and pays property taxes for you, the amount probably will be itemized on your monthly payment notice. If not, divide your annual tax bill by 12 to figure monthly costs.	Changes in your assessed valuation or the rate applied to the valuation both affect your monthly payment.	Home additions and improvements may result in a higher tax bill. So can rising costs of municipal services, as well as additional municipal services. Property taxes are also deductible on federal returns.
INSURANCE	If you pay premiums semi-annually, divide by six to figure monthly cost; if you pay annually, divide by 12.	Look for a pattern in previous increases and apply it to your projected costs. Your agent may know about increases in the offing.	To make sure your homeowners' policy provides adequate coverage, compare it annually to the value of your house. You may discover that your property is under-insured.
UPKEEP AND REPAIR	Untracked and forgotten cash expenditures might mean you're paying a lot more than what you think you are.	Besides inflationary effects, be sure to take into account anything that's due for replacement or major repairs, such as a roof, siding, or a driveway.	If you're contemplating an improvement, consider whether it will diminish or add to upkeep costs. Extra money spent on low-maintenance siding, for example, could be more than justified by paint jobs you wouldn't need.
UTILITIES	Present monthly costs could be distorted by utility-figured estimated bills, delayed bills, and bimonthly billings. Be alert for them.	Utility company petitions for increases are usually well publicized. Take note of them when figuring projections. Consumer groups often can predict any increases in rates.	As with maintenance and repair, conservation-oriented improvements can be cost-effective. Some utilities offer energy audits that can help you cut costs.

WHICH IMPROVEMENTS PAY OFF WHEN YOU SELL?

Any home improvement makes sense if it makes your family happy. And if it pleases *your* family, it will probably please another family, too. But don't delude yourself that you're going to get back every dollar you invest in improvements. Here's why—and what you can realistically expect to recover from typical improvements.

When you add to an existing house the addition almost always costs more than it would have if you had included it when the house was built. With a room addition, for example, you pay not only for the design and construction of the room itself, but also for the way it fits onto the rest of the house. An opening will have to be cut and special structural problems may need to be solved.

What's more, new-home builders can generally buy materials in greater quantities and at a better discount than remodelers can; often builders use labor more economically as well.

Inflation enters in, too. Even if all other factors were equal, that room addition you build today is going to cost a lot more than it would have had you included it when you built your house 20, 10, or even five years ago.

What are neighboring homes selling for?
Finally, you have to put yourself in the shoes of the prospective buyer. Let's say a buyer has a choice between your three-bedroom house and a comparable three-bedroom house down the street. The other seller's is priced at $100,000 because that's a typical selling price for three-bedroom homes in your area. You expect to sell yours for $120,000 because in addition to the usual appreciation, you added a third bedroom a few years ago at considerable expense.

Does the prospective buyer care about that? No. That person wants a well-maintained three-bedroom home in your neighborhood and isn't willing to pay $20,000 above the market price merely because one of your three bedrooms is

newer and more costly than the others.

Still, a third bedroom is a plus. Under most circumstances a three-bedroom house will sell much faster than a two-bedroom house. This doesn't mean the more bedrooms the merrier, however. Often houses with more than three bedrooms don't sell well at all. Many families don't need a fourth bedroom and consequently aren't willing to pay extra for one.

Don't over-improve
To a great extent the value of your house is determined by the average value of the other houses in the neighborhood. Say, for example, your house is in an area where the average selling price is $80,000. If the market value of your house is at or above that level you'd be well advised not to spend a substantial amount on improvements unless you're convinced you'll never want to live anywhere else. People who can afford a more expensive house usually want it located in a neighborhood of more expensive homes.

There are exceptions, of course. If your house is in an area of rapidly rising values—where large numbers of owners are spending heavily on improvements—the usual rules might not apply. This often happens in older city neighborhoods that have bottomed out, then come back because ambitious homeowners have bought run-down but solid houses and renovated them. In these cases, extensively remodeled houses can sell for a good deal more than the sum

of the purchase price and the cost of improvements.

Best bets
As you can see in the table *opposite*, improvements that pay off the most are the so-called "big four"—kitchen, bath, bedroom, and family room. Others that traditionally have paid off well include central air conditioning, fireplaces, and two-car garages, though a garage may not boost value appreciably in climates where you can get by with only a carport. Air conditioning and fireplaces seem to make economic sense even in areas where actual need is not particularly great. Figure a 50 to 75 percent return for air conditioning, probably half that for a fireplace unless you've invested only a few hundred dollars in a freestanding model. Large stone fireplaces seldom come even close to recouping their cost, though they make a home easier to sell.

Taking a chance
Those improvements least likely to produce a reasonable return for the money include frills such as swimming pools and tennis courts. Many prospective buyers tend to view them as troublesome and expensive to maintain and, in the case of a swimming pool, dangerous as well.

Neither does a basement rec room command much these days. Buyers who want a place to relax usually prefer to have something a little more upscale—and upstairs.

Be wary, too, of a garage conversion. A prospective buyer might prefer the garage, especially if the conversion has been amateurishly executed. If fact, any improvement that hasn't been done right will detract from, not add to, the value of your house.

VALUING HOME IMPROVEMENTS

	TYPICAL COST	POTENTIAL RETURN	SPECIAL NOTES
THE BIG FOUR			
Kitchen	$2,500 to $25,000	The big four probably will return at least 50 percent of initial investment; often they return 75 percent or more. Much depends on how well a job is executed, how it coordinates with the rest of the house, and how the improved house relates in price to others in the neighborhood.	People tend to go overboard on kitchen improvements. If you spend more than 10 percent of the value of your house, don't expect a commensurate jump in resale value. Second baths are almost always a good investment. So are third bedrooms and family rooms, unless they have been added at the sacrifice of a garage.
Bath	$1,000-$5,000		
Bedroom	$10,000-$25,000		
Family room	$10,000-$25,000		
ENERGY AND COMFORT			
Insulation	$500-$2,000	Energy-conserving improvements can only continue to do better in terms of resale value as energy costs rise and consumers become more energy-conscious.	Proportion is important. If you've added a $15,000 solar collector to a $40,000 house, your percentage return will be disappointing. The same goes for an ungainly power-generating windmill in a suburban backyard. Central air conditioning probably will pay off better than any of the other improvements. A fireplace is a good selling point, but a poor performer, generally, in terms of financial return.
Storm windows	$1,000-$5,000		
Air conditioning	$1,500-$15,000		
Fireplace or wood stove	$500-$5,000		
Solar/wind power	$3,000-$25,000		
FRILLS			
Swimming pool	$2,500-$25,000	Frills such as those listed here generally pay off disappointingly unless the house is in an area where these amenities are expected. Otherwise, don't count on more than 25 percent resale return.	Some of these can have a negative effect on the value of a house, especially if buyers perceive them as dangerous or expensive to maintain. Best advice is to consider only the enjoyment they provide your own family and forget about resale value altogether.
Hot tub	$1,000-$5,000		
Tennis court	$10,000-$20,000		
Special landscaping	$2,500-$10,000		

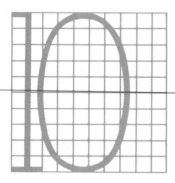

SHELVES

SPACE STRETCHERS YOU CAN MAKE

Does your house suffer from the too-full feeling that comes when you have more than it can comfortably hold? If so, the remedy is more storage. New storage requires space, of course, so look for unused places that might be hiding around your house. You'll uncover them if you work through room by room, keeping in mind projects like those in this chapter. You'll probably be surprised at how many bits of dead wall, ceiling, floor, and closet space you can turn into hardworking keeping places.

A shelving unit can do more than just store. This one incorporates a fold-up table and is 7 feet x 8½ feet x 14 inches. (Vary the dimensions to fit your room.) The shelves are 11½ inches deep to match standard drawers (not shown). For this unit you'll need:

2x2s: Eight 7-foot uprights; four 8½-foot lengths for the top and bottom; six 14½-inch shelf crosspieces; one 35-inch table crosspiece; two 30-inch table legs.

1x2s: One 24-inch table brace; 34 11½-inch shelf supports.

1x12s: 32-inch shelves.
Plywood: ¾x32x42 inches.
Plastic laminate: 32x48 inches.

Hardware: 34 3½x¼-inch

and five 5¼-inch hex bolts, nuts, and two washers per bolt; a 30-inch continuous hinge; a pair of 1½-inch butt hinges; a cabinet catch; one pound of 4d finish nails; one pint of contact cement.

Bolt crosspieces to four uprights using C-clamps and a ¼-inch drill bit. Bolt on top and bottom pieces and the four other uprights. Stand unit against wall; nail on 1x2 shelf supports at desired heights. Level the shelves.

Connect the two table legs with support brace; hinge them to table's underside. Bolt a crosspiece in front of the shelf at tabletop level; attach table with continuous hinge (table folds up over some shelves). Finish tabletop with plastic laminate or high-gloss enamel.

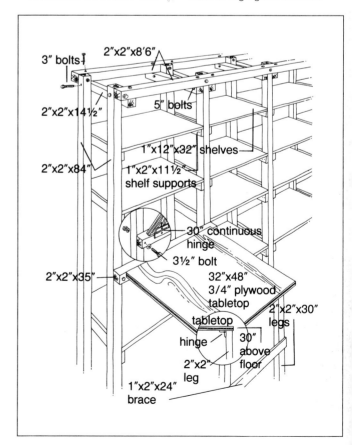

3" bolts
2"x2"x8'6"
2"x2"x14½"
5" bolts
1"x12"x32" shelves
2"x2"x84"
1"x2"x11½" shelf supports
30" continuous hinge
3½" bolt
32"x48" 3/4" plywood tabletop
2"x2"x35"
2"x2"x30" legs
tabletop hinge
30" above floor
2"x2" leg
1"x2"x24" brace

SHELVES
(continued)

To rid yourself of things underfoot, look overhead. There, with minimal cost, you can build shelves above head-bumping height.

New high-level storage will provide you the perfect place to stash seldom-used items, such as lightweight luggage (as shown *opposite bottom*); small boxes and files covered in paper or fabric, or painted to add to a room's decoration; yard goods and remnants that always seem to gather; extra linens and towels; or, to keep at hand, hobby supplies, camera gear, and slides.

Overhead shelves are versatile and will work well in just about any room in your home. In the kitchen, there's no better place for party supplies and picnic ware than an overhead shelf. And a long shelf over a bedroom window makes perfect storage for rarely used books. Even items such as correspondence files and small tool kits are all the more accessible if stored up high rather than stashed away in the garage or basement. Overhead shelves can do more than just store, however; they can display, too. Pottery and baskets or a doll collection will enliven a room just as much from on high as from down low on shelves or in glass cases.

Over a window

To re-create the handsome shelf *at right,* nail 1x2 cleats to the flanking walls. They'll provide ample support for bulky objects that are not heavy. Preassemble the shelf by connecting ¾-inch plywood and a 1½x3-inch dadoed edge strip. Screw the plywood at the sides and back to bottoms of the cleats, and nail on the edge strip.

A shelf more than 10 feet long will need extra support. A chain (use a decorative one if you want) will work well. Suspend it from the ceiling, preferably from a joist, and attach it to the middle of the edge strip.

Finish the shelf to harmonize with the room. If the room is wallpapered, paper the shelf bottom so the edge appears to float in midair.

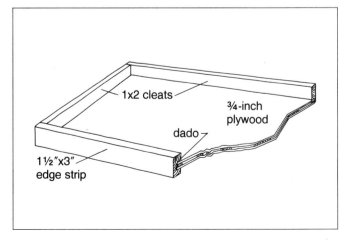

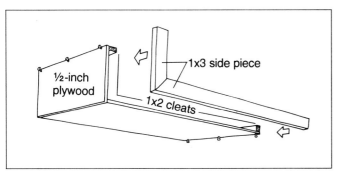

Here's an L-shape built-in that can solve problems all over the house—in bedrooms, the mud room, even the family room. You don't have to place the L over a doorway, although this often is the most convenient location. Wherever you place it, the shelf will be more accessible if you leave both sides open. (However, if you place it in a corner, reduce the unit's depth.)

If you can reach the top of your door, you can reach to the bottom of this shelf. To aid storage and retrieval, use a grocery grab-hook.

To build the unit, use ½-inch plywood for the main unit, with 1x2 cleats to attach it to a wall and the ceiling, and 1x3 side pieces for finish edges. Be sure to screw the ceiling cleat to one or more joists. Then attach the plywood unit to the cleats, and nail on the side pieces. To store heavy objects, reinforce the inside corner joint with another cleat by screwing through both plywood pieces.

To put the storage L over a door, remove the top piece of the door casing for working room to install the wall cleat. (Replace the casing when you're done.)

Stain or enamel the 1x3 to match the room's woodwork, or paint the whole unit the same color.

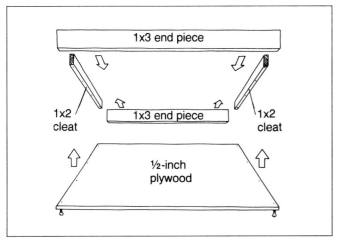

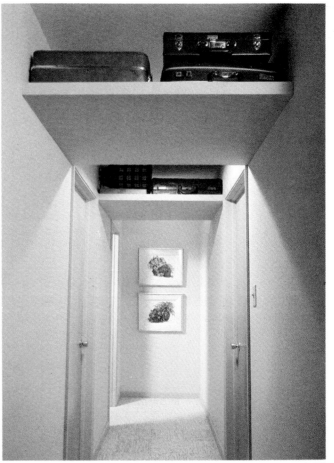

All too often, hallways are dismissed as just circulation space that's otherwise useless. But they're ideal places for storing the bulky luggage and boxes that clutter most bedroom closets. Install a platform at each end of the hall (or along its whole length). Leave about 3 feet of clear space between platforms for access. You'll never miss the space they use, and you'll barely notice them.

Like the L-unit, hall shelves are handier if you leave them open at both ends. If you put one end against a wall, reduce the unit's depth so stored items are easy to retrieve.

Use ½-inch plywood for the base. Nail 1x2 cleats to each wall as support; screw the plywood to the bottom of the cleats. Then nail the 1x3 end pieces onto the free edges to serve as retainer lips.

Highlight the units with contrasting paint, or let them blend with the rest of your decor.

DIVIDERS

If you have a large living space that always seems cluttered, perhaps the remedy is to cut the room into more manageable areas with a divider. Although you lose some floor space to the divider, you gain increased livability from the new areas. The rooms *above* and *opposite* show just how well this divide-to-conquer technique works.

When two are better than one

A large, undefined and unorganized room will serve you better when subdivided into smaller spaces that have well-defined duties. The room *above* aptly demonstrates this.

Once a tunnel-like living room in a 1938 bungalow, it always was hard to arrange well. Now it functions smoothly as separate living and dining areas. The new divider—the key alteration—doubles as traffic director and stowing space; it also supports the long, built-in sofa. Minimizing the need for supplementary storage furniture, cabinets beneath the divider's counter replace chests, shelves, and tables that otherwise would take up valuable living space.

Because the divider stops short of the ceiling, neither subdivided space feels cramped. A mirror high over the sofa further increases the airy open look of the whole area. A fine finishing touch, the niche on the divider's living-room side, showcases favorite accessories against a deep eggplant-colored background with downlights.

High and low drama

When subdividing a room, or adding on, look for opportunities to build storage dividers instead of ordinary partitions. Placing a new wing at a level different from that of the old rooms opens many possibilities, as shown *opposite*.

The add-on living room, *opposite above,* falls several feet below the dining room, *opposite below,* in the older section of the house. Where the house once ended, an open divider passes light from the new living room to the dining room. Two posts and a beam, now integrated into the mainly drywall divider, support the roof.

On the living-room side, *opposite above,* the lower part of the divider consists largely of bins for the family's stereo equipment, record collection, books, and magazines. On the dining-room side, *lower right,*

the divider has a built-in buffet and storage for china and silver. Inside, adjustable shelves accommodate all the tableware; another section stores liquor and serves as a bar.

The mirrored dining-room ceiling augments the raised area's natural light, and nightlighting from the border of clear-globe lamps. The mirrors also enhance the open flow of spaces. Sleek, white built-ins and a neutral living room rug create the perfect background for vividly colored armchairs, bold modern paintings, and the soft lines of plants.

(continued)

DIVIDERS
(continued)

A home fireplace sparks anyone's interest in a house. But many homes, especially small ones built since the late 1940s, often lack fireplaces. These same houses usually lack storage, too. If you're thinking about adding a fireplace, consider a project that addresses your storage problem as well; you might also gain a divider in the bargain.

Today's compact and versatile prefabricated fireplaces will fit almost anywhere. If shopping for one, look at "zero-clearance" fireplaces. These have double-wall construction and—unlike other units—don't require minimum distances from combustible materials. You can even build wood frames around some of these units (but follow the manufacturer's directions and local codes to the letter).

This new fireplace, *opposite,* divides a dining room from a remodeled living room. The fireplace exhibits a rich contrast of solids, voids, and projections. At the divider's end, a niche painted dark brown emphasizes the oak shelves. In the living room, a set of adjustable shelves sits in a white niche, repeating the trim of the fireplace hearth and the broad oak band above it. Back of the fireplace, on the dining-room side, more recessed storage of a similar design fills the divider.

Mexican paver tiles surround the fireplace opening and cover the raised L-shape hearth. This hearth not only is a design "plus," it also serves the necessary function of meeting code requirements for a noncombustible hearth: typically these call for a fireproof surface at least 16 inches deep and at least 16 inches wider than the fireplace opening.

Many people like wide-open spaces. If a room is too wide and open, however, it lacks focus. With no clear reference point, the room can only generate a vague sense that something is missing.

What's missing, of course, are defined boundaries and a human scale. Both help give a feeling of comfort and privacy. *Above,* a partial wall permits a view of the whole space be-yond from either side, yet sets up a cozy enclosure. The geometric drywall divider incorporates a supporting beam and separates the sleeping area from the rest of a large master-bedroom suite. A foot-wide wood counter surface holds books close at hand.

Behind the bed, more built-ins for a telephone, bed lamp, family photographs, and books and magazines protectively surround the built-in platform and add some features of a study. The picture window offers an expansive view of the outside, and highlights the snugness of this attic-turned-retreat.

A divider like this also would work as a dressing table, with, for example, storage in the horizontal section and a hinged dropleaf mirror attached to one section of the counter. Another section of the counter and its underneath storage could convert to a writing desk or a sewing corner.

ORGANIZING
HALLS AND CLOSETS

A back-entry hall, usually undeveloped though heavily trafficked, makes a prime candidate for a mud room. All you need are a few built-ins.

At left, foul-weather gear now finds a permanent home —no more delays while somebody hunts for a lost umbrella or strayed galoshes. Child-size benches, upholstered and painted a dirt-hiding color, store boots in slide-out bins. Casters make it easy even for children to roll the bins in and out, encouraging their use by the family's notorious litterers. Open shelves organize gloves, scarves, and sports equipment. And wall-mounted plastic hooks corral jackets, overcoats, and raincoats.

Even if you've already put the back hall to work (or your house lacks one), you still may find an untamed frontier in your home—inside the front hall. There you often have to sidestep an unwieldy tangle of boots and coats flung on the floor.

Below left, cubby holes, pegs, and baskets catch hallway clutter. The wall pegs latch onto coats and scarves; a series of little baskets (just out of the photo at the right) hang wet mittens near a radiator for drying; and floor-to-ceiling cubbyholes hold just about everything else: sweaters, caps, tennis rackets, running shoes, boots, easy-to-lose small items. A closet rod across the space beneath a stairway handles jackets, and bulky sports gear stows under the jackets.

Pocket doors slide into walls on either side, giving access to the whole closet. To keep maintenance at a minimum, quarry tile, impervious to mud, stretches across the hall and into the closet.

Most modern kitchens would have more useful storage space if they had pantries like the old-fashioned ones in old houses. But if you're fortunate enough to have a closet or alcove near your kitchen, you can transform it into a large, hardworking pantry. And putting kitchen equipment so close at hand in your pantry will help turn cooking chores into cooking pleasures.

If you have any blank wall space in or near your kitchen, you can add floor-to-ceiling shelves to set up a small pantry. But an alcove or closet offers space for a full-scale pantry. Your new pantry surely will become a home for bulky casseroles, large platters, baskets, bulky dry goods, extra vases, serving dishes, small appliances—everything you want within easy reach but stored neatly away.

At right, the central shelves, 11 inches deep, are made of laminated wood edged in birch. At the sides, behind sliding doors, 9-inch shelves hold canned goods and packaged foods. With these shallow shelves, everything is visible; nothing gets lost. Above the shelves, a birch soffit visually ties together the three sections of storage.

To set up shelves for lightweight items, you'll need supporting cleats nailed to the walls at shelf ends. Long shelves, or those intended for heavy goods, will require metal brackets secured to the wall.

Also put up wall pegs to hold aprons. This will keep them from being thrown into drawers to mildew, or draped over chairs, eventually to drop to the floor.

WHERE TO GO FOR MORE INFORMATION

Better Homes and Gardens® Books
Would you like to learn more about decorating, remodeling, or maintaining your home? These Better Homes and Gardens® books can help.

Better Homes and Gardens®
NEW DECORATING BOOK
How to translate ideas into workable solutions for every room in your home. Choosing a style; furniture arrangements; windows, walls, and ceilings; floors; lighting; and accessories. 433 color photos, 76 how-to illustrations, 432 pages.

Better Homes and Gardens®
COMPLETE GUIDE TO HOME REPAIR,
MAINTENANCE, & IMPROVEMENT
Inside your home, outside your home, your home's systems, basics you should know. Anatomy and step-by-step drawings illustrate components, tools, techniques, and finishes. 515 how-to techniques; 75 charts; 2,734 illustrations; 552 pages.

Better Homes and Gardens®
COMPLETE GUIDE TO GARDENING
A comprehensive guide for beginners and experienced gardeners. Houseplants, lawns and landscaping, trees and shrubs, greenhouses, insects and diseases. 461 color photos, 434 how-to illustrations, 37 charts, 552 pages.

Better Homes and Gardens®
STEP-BY-STEP
BASIC PLUMBING
Getting to know your system, solving plumbing problems, making plumbing improvements, plumbing basics and procedures. 42 projects, 200 illustrations, 96 pages.

Better Homes and Gardens®
STEP-BY-STEP
BASIC WIRING
Getting to know your system, solving electrical problems, making electrical improvements, electrical basics and procedures. 22 projects, 286 illustrations, 96 pages.

Better Homes and Gardens®
STEP-BY-STEP
BASIC CARPENTRY
Setting up shop, choosing tools and building materials, mastering construction techniques, building boxes, hanging shelves, framing walls, installing drywall and paneling. 10 projects, 191 illustrations, 96 pages.

Better Homes and Gardens®
STEP-BY-STEP
MASONRY & CONCRETE
Choosing tools and materials; planning masonry projects; working with concrete; working with brick, block, and stone; special-effect projects. 10 projects, 200 drawings, 96 pages.

Better Homes and Gardens®
STEP-BY-STEP
HOUSEHOLD REPAIRS
Basic tools for repair jobs, repairing walls and ceilings, floors and stairs, windows, doors, electrical and plumbing items. 200 illustrations, 96 pages.

Other Sources of Information
Most professional associations publish lists of their members and will be happy to send you their booklets upon request. They may also offer informational and educational material for the asking.

American Gas Association
1515 Wilson Blvd.
Arlington, VA 22209

American Hardboard Association (AHA)
887-B Wilmette Road
Palatine, IL 60067

American Home Lighting Institute
230 N. Michigan Avenue
Chicago, IL 60601

Association of Home Appliance Manufacturers (AHAM)
20 N. Wacker Drive
Chicago, IL 60606

Cellulose Manufacturers Association (CMA)
5908 Columbia Pike
Baileys Crossroads, VA 22041

Exterior Insulation Manufacturers Association (EIMA)
1000 Vermont Avenue, NW Suite 1200
Washington, DC 20005

Major Appliance Consumer Action Panel (MACAP)
20 N. Wacker Dr.
Chicago, IL 60606

National Association of the Remodeling Industry (NARI)
11 E. 44th St.
New York, NY 10017

National Housewares Manufacturers Association (NHMA)
1130 Merchandise Mart
Chicago, IL 60654

National Kitchen and Bath Association (NKBA)
114 Main Street
Hackettstown, NJ 07840

Tile Council of America
Box 326
Princeton, NJ 08540

ACKNOWLEDGMENTS

**Archtects
and Designers**

The following is a listing by page of the interior designers, architects, and project designers whose work appears in this book.

Pages 6-7
Robert K. Lewis Assoc.
Pages 8-9
John Seals
Pages 10-11
Suzy Taylor
Pages 14-15
The Design Concern
Pages 16-17
Amisano and Stegmaier
Pages 18-19
Maurice Finegold
Pages 20-21
Suzy Taylor
Pages 24-25
Robert Rutemiller and Wynn Westerman
Pages 26-27
Robert E. Dittmer
Pages 28-29
Harold Langell
Pages 30-31
Jack Wozniak and Assoc.
Pages 32-33
Pamela Hughes of The H. Chambers Co.
Pages 34-35
Ast-Dagdelen Architects; Marvin Ullman
Pages 36-37
Don Vermeland, Svedberg-Vermeland Architects
Pages 38-39
Ron Sorenson; Pamela Pennington
Pages 40-41
Elaine Protass/Muriel Hebert
Pages 42-43
UNO/ASID Student Group,

University of Nebraska; Carol Stegmeister
Pages 44-45
Jim and Sharon Stoebner; Sandra Shapiro
Pages 48-49
Suzy Taylor
Pages 52-53
Marlene Grant
Pages 54-55
Sudie Woodson Interiors; Judi Hinkle
Pages 56-57
Tom Boccia
Pages 58-59
Louisa Cowan, Armstrong Design Center; Fisher Friedman Associates
Pages 60-61
Richard Taylor, The H. Chambers Co.
Pages 62-63
The Design Concern
Pages 64-65
Robert Filler
Pages 66-67
Louisa Cowan, Armstrong Design Center; Tony Torrice
Pages 68-69
Laurel Lund and Robert E. Dittmer
Pages 74-75
Barbara R. Kapp
Pages 76-77
Jay Alpert
Pages 80-81
Wilkes and Faulkner
Pages 82-83
Word and Cummings;

S. Stewart Farnet
Pages 84-85
Finegold and Bullis
Pages 86-87
John A. Kelly
Pages 88-89
Douglas Dahlin
Pages 92-93
The Design Concern; Judith Ross, Trade Winds, Inc.
Pages 94-95
John and Joanna Baymiller; Harry Jacobs
Pages 98-99
Daryl Hansen
Pages 100-101
Amisano and Stegmaier
Pages 102-103
Kemp Mooney; Michael E. Collins
Pages 104-105
Parker C. Folse; Gerald Thomlin
Pages 106-107
Jena Hall
Pages 110-111
Stephen Glassman
Pages 112-113
Amisano and Stegmaier
Pages 114-115
Lynn Nelson and Jennifer Kelly
Pages 116-117
Rick Millikan, Abrams, Millikan, & Kent
Pages 120-121
John Busby; Emilio Pittzrelli
Pages 122-123
H. Randal Roark; Fred Bainbridge
Pages 124-125
Don Zygas, Pace Interiors; DHL Associates, construction
Pages 126-127

James Miles
Pages 128-129
David Durrant
Pages 130-131
William B. Remick
Pages 142-143
The Design Concern
Pages 144-145
Robert C. London; Michael L. Smith
Pages 146-147
Shawmy Noily; Joel D'Orazio
Pages 148-149
Don Vermeland; Don Roberts, Roberts Associates, Architects, Planners

**Photographers
and Illustrators**

We extend our thanks to the following photographers and illustrators, whose creative talents and technical skills contributed to this book.

Ernest Braun
Ross Chapple
Mike Dieter
Harry Hartman
Hedrich-Blessing
Bill Helms
Thomas Hooper
William N. Hopkins
Fred Lyon
E. Alan McGee
Marine Arts
Maris/Semel
Frank Lotz Miller
Jordan Miller
Carson Ode
Jessie Walker

STRETCHING LIVING SPACE

TEMPLATES TO HELP YOU PLAN

UPHOLSTERED FURNITURE AND BEDDING

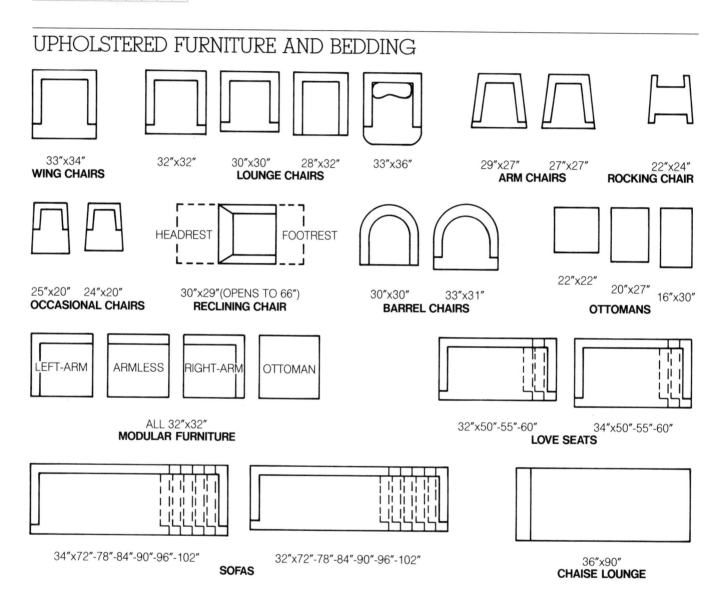

33"x34"
WING CHAIRS

32"x32"   30"x30"   28"x32"
LOUNGE CHAIRS

33"x36"

29"x27"   27"x27"
ARM CHAIRS

22"x24"
ROCKING CHAIR

25"x20"   24"x20"
OCCASIONAL CHAIRS

HEADREST   FOOTREST

30"x29"(OPENS TO 66")
RECLINING CHAIR

30"x30"   33"x31"
BARREL CHAIRS

22"x22"
20"x27"   16"x30"
OTTOMANS

LEFT-ARM   ARMLESS   RIGHT-ARM   OTTOMAN

ALL 32"x32"
MODULAR FURNITURE

32"x50"-55"-60"
34"x50"-55"-60"
LOVE SEATS

34"x72"-78"-84"-90"-96"-102"
32"x72"-78"-84"-90"-96"-102"
SOFAS

36"x90"
CHAISE LOUNGE

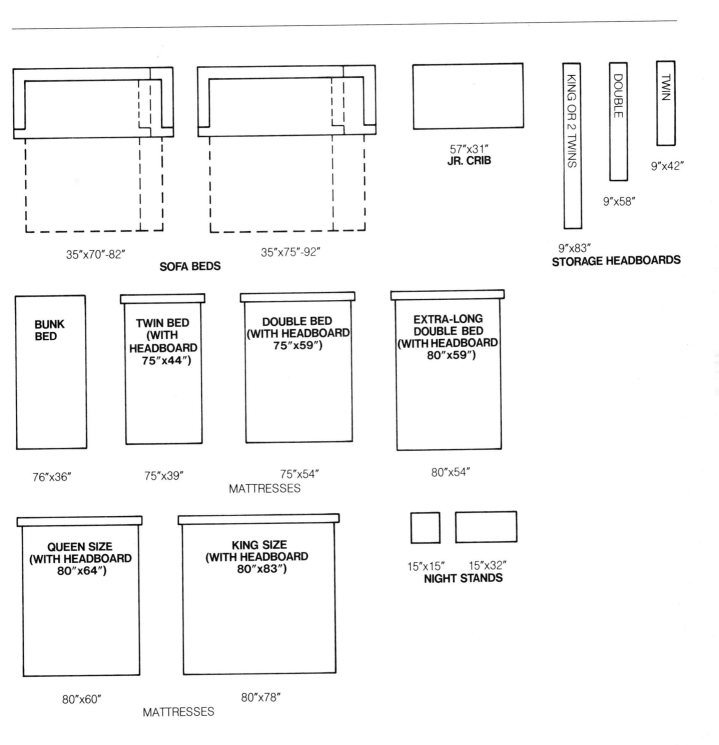

57"x31"
JR. CRIB

KING OR 2 TWINS

9"x83"

DOUBLE

9"x58"

TWIN

9"x42"

STORAGE HEADBOARDS

35"x70"-82"

35"x75"-92"

SOFA BEDS

BUNK
BED

76"x36"

TWIN BED
(WITH
HEADBOARD
75"x44")

75"x39"

DOUBLE BED
(WITH HEADBOARD
75"x59")

75"x54"

MATTRESSES

EXTRA-LONG
DOUBLE BED
(WITH HEADBOARD
80"x59")

80"x54"

QUEEN SIZE
(WITH HEADBOARD
80"x64")

80"x60"

KING SIZE
(WITH HEADBOARD
80"x83")

80"x78"

MATTRESSES

15"x15"   15"x32"
NIGHT STANDS

153

TEMPLATES
TO HELP YOU
PLAN

TABLES AND DINING ROOM PIECES

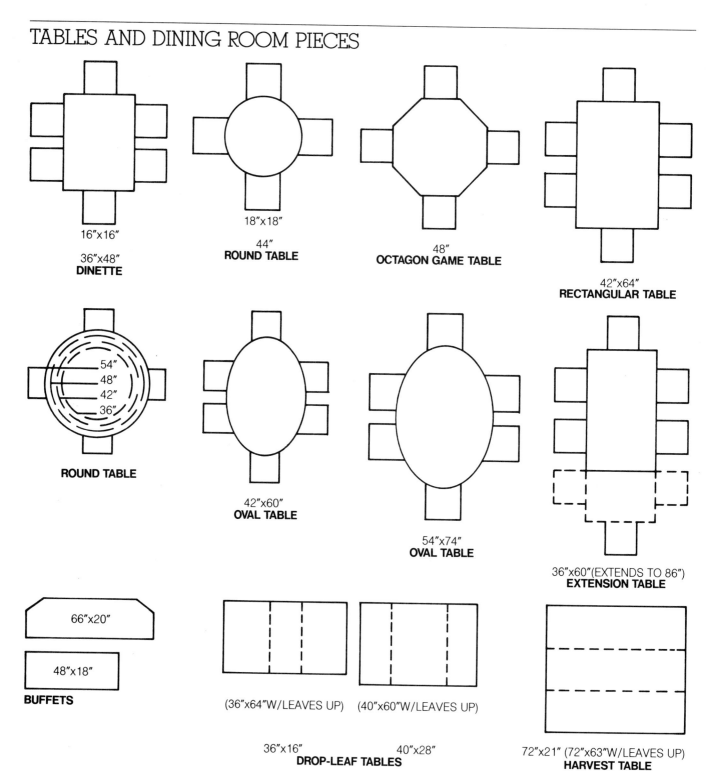

16"x16"

36"x48"
DINETTE

18"x18"

44"
ROUND TABLE

48"
OCTAGON GAME TABLE

42"x64"
RECTANGULAR TABLE

54"
48"
42"
36"

ROUND TABLE

42"x60"
OVAL TABLE

54"x74"
OVAL TABLE

36"x60"(EXTENDS TO 86")
EXTENSION TABLE

66"x20"

48"x18"

BUFFETS

(36"x64"W/LEAVES UP)

(40"x60"W/LEAVES UP)

36"x16"

40"x28"
DROP-LEAF TABLES

72"x21" (72"x63"W/LEAVES UP)
HARVEST TABLE

INTERCHANGEABLE STORAGE PIECES AND SPECIAL PIECES

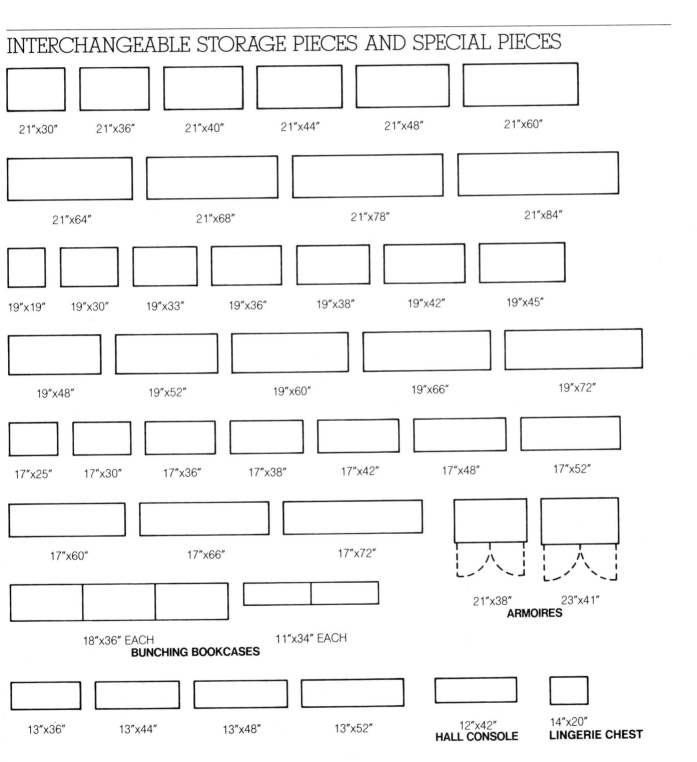

21"x30" 21"x36" 21"x40" 21"x44" 21"x48" 21"x60"

21"x64" 21"x68" 21"x78" 21"x84"

19"x19" 19"x30" 19"x33" 19"x36" 19"x38" 19"x42" 19"x45"

19"x48" 19"x52" 19"x60" 19"x66" 19"x72"

17"x25" 17"x30" 17"x36" 17"x38" 17"x42" 17"x48" 17"x52"

17"x60" 17"x66" 17"x72"

21"x38" 23"x41"
ARMOIRES

18"x36" EACH
BUNCHING BOOKCASES

11"x34" EACH

13"x36" 13"x44" 13"x48" 13"x52"

12"x42"
HALL CONSOLE

14"x20"
LINGERIE CHEST

STRETCHING LIVING SPACE

TEMPLATES TO HELP YOU PLAN

OCCASIONAL TABLES, DESKS, AND SPECIAL PIECES

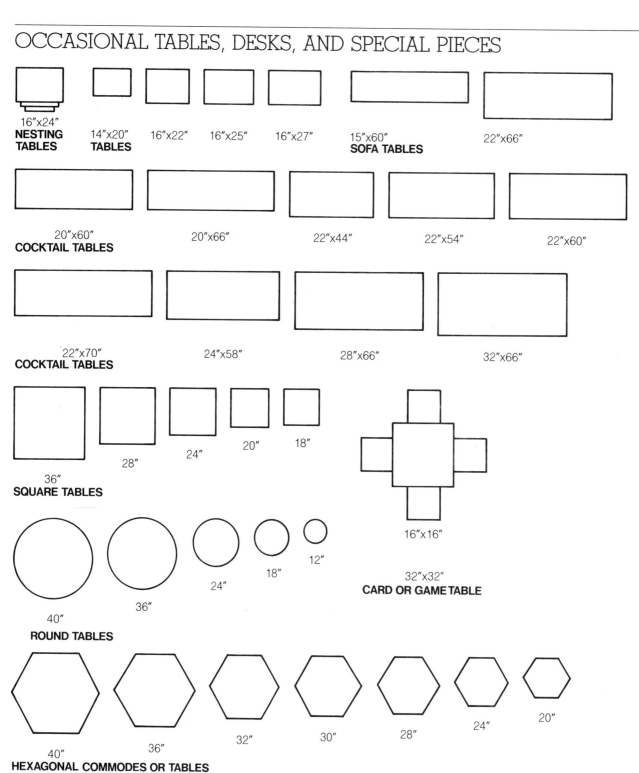

16"x24"
NESTING TABLES

14"x20"
TABLES

16"x22" 16"x25" 16"x27"

15"x60"
SOFA TABLES

22"x66"

20"x60"
COCKTAIL TABLES

20"x66" 22"x44" 22"x54" 22"x60"

22"x70"
COCKTAIL TABLES

24"x58" 28"x66" 32"x66"

36"
SQUARE TABLES

28" 24" 20" 18"

16"x16"

32"x32"
CARD OR GAME TABLE

40"
ROUND TABLES

36" 24" 18" 12"

40" 36" 32" 30" 28" 24" 20"
HEXAGONAL COMMODES OR TABLES

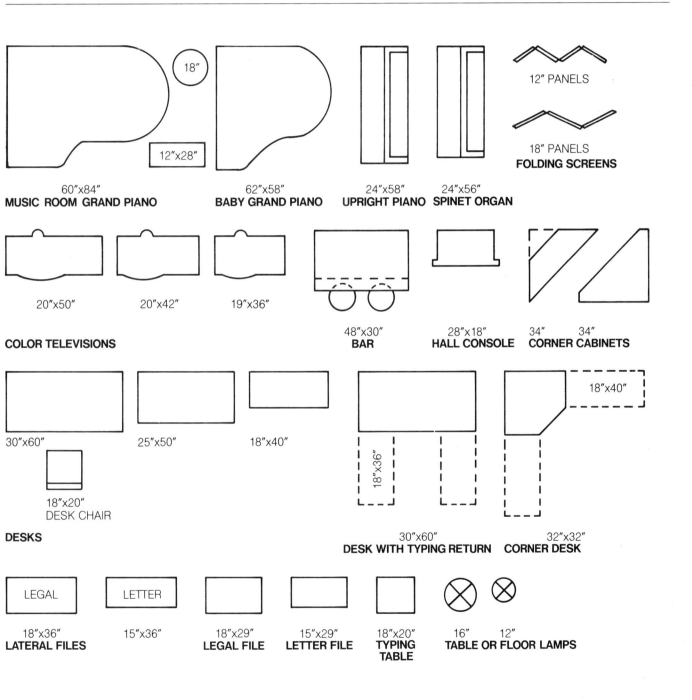

12" PANELS

18" PANELS
FOLDING SCREENS

60"x84"
MUSIC ROOM GRAND PIANO

62"x58"
BABY GRAND PIANO

24"x58"
UPRIGHT PIANO

24"x56"
SPINET ORGAN

20"x50"   20"x42"   19"x36"

COLOR TELEVISIONS

48"x30"
BAR

28"x18"
HALL CONSOLE

34"   34"
CORNER CABINETS

30"x60"   25"x50"   18"x40"

18"x20"
DESK CHAIR

DESKS

18"x36"

30"x60"
DESK WITH TYPING RETURN

18"x40"

32"x32"
CORNER DESK

LEGAL   LETTER

18"x36"
LATERAL FILES

15"x36"

18"x29"
LEGAL FILE

15"x29"
LETTER FILE

18"x20"
TYPING TABLE

16"   12"
TABLE OR FLOOR LAMPS

Page numbers in *italics* refer to photographs or illustrated test.